W9-AQI-416

FOL 3

Rebecca Danger

THE BIG BOOK OF
Knitted Monsters

Mischievous, Lovable Toys

Martingale®
& COMPANY

The Big Book of Knitted Monsters:
Mischievous, Lovable Toys
© 2011 by Rebecca Danger

Martingale®
& COMPANY

Martingale & Company
19021 120th Ave. NE, Ste. 102
Bothell, WA 98011-9511 USA
www.martingale-pub.com

No part of this product may be reproduced in any form, unless otherwise stated, in which case reproduction is limited to the use of the purchaser. The written instructions, photographs, designs, projects, and patterns are intended for the personal, noncommercial use of the retail purchaser and are under federal copyright laws; they are not to be reproduced by any electronic, mechanical, or other means, including informational storage or retrieval systems, for commercial use. Permission is granted to photocopy patterns for the personal use of the retail purchaser. Attention teachers: Martingale & Company encourages you to use this book for teaching, subject to the restrictions stated above.

The information in this book is presented in good faith, but no warranty is given nor results guaranteed. Since Martingale & Company has no control over choice of materials or procedures, the company assumes no responsibility for the use of this information.

Printed in China
16 15 14 13 12 11   8 7 6 5 4 3 2

Library of Congress Cataloging-in-Publication Data is available upon request.

ISBN: 978-1-60468-009-6

Dedication

To James, Abbey, and Lucy Danger: you're my family and my everything. And to my Grandma Lillian, who taught me to knit and without whom none of this would have been possible.

Mission Statement

Dedicated to providing quality products and service to inspire creativity.

Credits

President & CEO ✳ Tom Wierzbicki
Editor in Chief ✳ Mary V. Green
Managing Editor ✳ Tina Cook
Developmental Editor ✳ Karen Costello Soltys
Technical Editor ✳ Ursula Reikes
Copy Editor ✳ Sheila Chapman Ryan
Design Director ✳ Stan Green
Production Manager ✳ Regina Girard
Cover & Text Designer ✳ Adrienne Smitke
Photographer ✳ Brent Kane

Acknowledgments

I want to take a minute to thank everyone that made my first book a possibility:

The amazing folks at Martingale & Company;

my husband, Mr. Danger, for putting up with me while I worked and putting up with a million monsters in a tiny house;

my family and friends who actually sounded like they were interested in everything I said even though all I talked about was my book and nothing else for a year;

the yarn companies who so graciously sent yarn to become monsters;

Linda Roghaar and Vicki Stiefel for their help and support;

my devoted customers for being so awesome;

and the baristas at the Lynden, Washington, Starbucks (since no monsters would have been knit without a whole bunch of espresso).

From the bottom of my heart, thank you, thank you, thank you.

Contents

Introduction

Hello and welcome to the wacky world of Rebecca Danger and Danger Crafts! In your hands you're holding my very first book of patterns and the information you need to make an entire house full of knitted monsters. My house is full to the gills with monsters, which means that I smile every day since everywhere I look a bright monster face is smiling back at me. I wish that same joy for you as well, and I hope you will quickly fill your home with smiling armies of knitted monsters!

The secret is out: I'm completely obsessed with knitting toys, and in particular monsters. I love to knit toys: they are quick and relatively easy, there is no concern with fit and gauge, and they don't use much yarn. Plus, they make the cutest finished knitted items that people can't help but smile and laugh at when they see them. Unfortunately for me, people seem to laugh at the sweaters I knit too—I just welcome their laughter much more when they are looking at my monsters. I hope you enjoy knitting my monsters as much as I do.

Wishing you big monster smiles and hours of knitting fun.

~ Rebecca Danger

General Monster Knitting Guidelines

You should know some basic things before you dive too deep into knitting monsters. So, roll up your sleeves, read through these guidelines, grab some yarn and needles, and get your knit on!

Hello, Lover: Yarn

Knitting monsters is a great way to use up yarn in your stash, since just about anything will produce a really great-looking monster. Plus, since you only need a couple hundred yards for most of my monsters, I'm sure you have a couple balls of something that you bought just because it was pretty. Or on sale. Or both. I think every single knitter is guilty of this, but you don't have to feel guilty anymore! Now you can walk through any yarn store and buy with abandon since you can always make a monster out of it.

That being said, my favorite monster-making yarns are Berroco Comfort and Cascade Yarns 220 100% Peruvian Highland Wool or Cascade Yarns 220 100% Superwash Wool. I like these because they knit up well with a single strand (or two strands held together), they take stuffing well, they're pretty inexpensive, they have great color palettes, and they just look good finished. But, just as much as I like the Comfort and the 220, I love all kinds of other yarns, too. Try Cascade Magnum on size 13 needles for a really gigantic monster, or any Spud and Chloë yarn for a big punch of color.

My personal belief for monster yarn is the bulkier the better: I tend to avoid working on needles below a U.S. size 4 since needles get too pokey for me at that point. But, I've seen lots of my patterns worked on sock and other light yarns and I must say they come out just as cute as the big guys. I like to double strand yarns too, since I can knit on larger needles, plus it often gives you an entirely different feeling than knitting with a single strand of the same yarn. Honestly, I prefer to double strand Cascade 220 rather than use a single strand. I swear it looks and acts better as a bulkier yarn.

Knitting monsters is all about what feels right and what's fun. I encourage you to try a bunch of yarns until you have a repertoire of yarns that you really love to work with and that give you the monster results you desire. Plus, experimenting with yarns means buying more yarn, and what knitter isn't just in it for the yarn, right? Refer to "Standard Yarn-Weight System" on page 12 for guidance when making substitutions.

What's the Deal with Gauge?

For those of you who hate gauging as much as I do, knitting a toy is a perfect project for you. One of the greatest things about toys is gauge doesn't matter! Simply use smaller needles than those recommended for your yarn to create a tight-knit fabric so that the stuffing doesn't show through. My rule of thumb is to go down two or three needle sizes from the smallest recommended needle size for your yarn. For example, I knit my Cascade Yarns 220 100% Peruvian Highland Wool, which is recommended to be knit on size 7 or 8 needles, on size 5 needles instead. Or, I knit a double strand of Cascade 220 on size 9 needles.

This is by no means a hard-and-fast rule on gauge. Just like everything else in this book, it's really up to you. I can look at a yarn and get a general feel for what size needles it's going to look best on, and I'm sure you'll be able to as well when you get a couple knit monsters under your belt. Be flexible and don't be afraid to pull something out and start again if it doesn't look right. It's your monster, so make it your way!

And I Will Knit 5,000 Miles: Yardage

There's nothing worse than running out of yarn with just one arm or ear left to go. I'm notorious for this and I apparently don't learn from my mistakes. For the monsters in this book I ended up running out of yarn when making at least three samples, which left me very cranky to say the least. So, let's make sure you don't share my same issue, shall we?

The recommended yardage for the patterns in this book is for a size 4 to 9 needle range. Yes, you can *probably* sneak a monster through on size 10 needles, but just to be safe, I would add an extra 20 to 40 yards if you're knitting on needles that large and I'd add even more, up to 100 yards over the recommended, if you're using anything larger. Here's how it works: smaller needles mean you will need the low end of the recommended yardage, bigger needles mean you will need the higher end of the recommended yardage. You got it? And seriously, just buy that extra skein. Worse-case scenario you can make a striped monster in the future, or you can probably make a Coco (page 51) out of your extra yarn, since she's a small monster. Extra yarn just means you can knit extra monsters, and the more monsters the merrier, right?

The Joy of Magic Loop

I recommend using the Magic Loop method for most of my patterns. I love the Magic Loop method; it's my preferred knitting-in-the-round technique. It's quick, easy, you can use one size of needle for everything, there's no danger of slipped stitches from your double-pointed needles, you don't have to transfer to double-pointed needles as you decrease, it transports easily, it's more fun (seriously)—I could go on and on. Many people find Magic Loop to be, well, rather terrifying, and I respect that. Though I encourage you to take the plunge and learn the Magic Loop method, all of my patterns can easily be knit on a set of double-pointed needles or a small-circumference circular needle instead (you'll have to be the judge depending on how big or small your project is).

Let's break down the steps for Magic Loop and make it easy. Grab a 36" or longer circular knitting needle with a flexible cable. Cast on your stitches as you would normally.

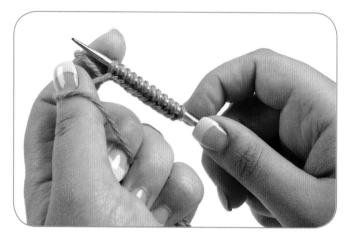

Now, slide the stitches to the center of the cable and find the center point to divide the stitches in half. Pull the cable out at this point.

Slide the stitches from the cable up onto the needles, with half the stitches on the front needle and half the stitches on the back needle. The working yarn should be coming from the stitches on the back needle.

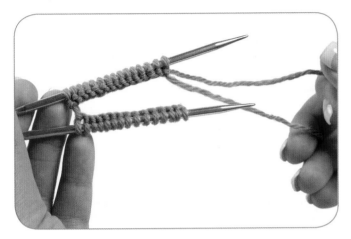

With the cast-on edge facing inward to avoid twisted stitches, get ready to knit in the round. But, before you start, pull the back needle out so that about half the cable is sticking out to the left-hand side and the other half of the cable is sticking out to the right-hand side.

Now, with the working yarn over and behind the cable of the back needle, knit across the stitches on the front needle. (I generally place a marker about two to four stitches in so I know this is the beginning of my round.) Once you get to the end of that needle, pull the needles so that all the stitches are back on the needles.

Turn your work around, pull the back needle out again as you did to start, and with the working yarn over and behind the cable of the back needle, knit across the second needle of stitches.

Eureka! You're Magic Looping! Now do this 1,000 times until you're really comfortable with it.

Get in the (Backward) Loop

Can you really cast on backward? Of course you can! Backward-loop cast on is a quick and easy cast on that I love because it makes it a cinch to add stitches mid-round or mid-row. It's as easy as doing the monster mash. Grab your working yarn, make a loop, and just slide it onto your needle as shown. Forget any fancy footwork; just repeat as many times as you need for the required number of stitches.

The Legs to Body Situation

The hardest part of my patterns is moving on from the legs to the body on the monsters where the body/legs/head are all knit as one unit (for examples, see Kat, Gort, and Hugo). Here's the skinny.

When you're done with the first leg, including the backward-loop cast-on stitches, transfer these stitches to your circular needle by putting half the leg stitches on the front needle and half the leg stitches plus the cast-on stitches on the back needle, with the cast-on stitches toward the right end of the back needle.

Make a second leg and cut your yarn, leaving a 10" tail for sewing up at the end. Divide the second leg's stitches onto just two of your double-pointed needles, with half the leg stitches on one needle and half the leg stitches plus the cast-on stitches on the other needle. Now, transfer these stitches onto the circular needle just as you have them divided on your double-pointed needles, putting half the leg stitches plus the cast-on stitches on the *front* needle and half the leg stitches on the *back* needle. There will be cast-on stitches on both needles between the first and second leg. You now have a new beginning of the round in the middle of your monster's second leg.

Now that you've transferred the stitches to your circular needle from knitting the two legs individually, you have cut all ties you have to the legs—in other words, your yarn. This will set you up to easily get your decreases directly on the sides without too much tricky counting, especially if you use the Magic Loop method to knit the body. See, there is some sanity in all of my monster madness!

To Everything, Turn, Turn, Turn

Many of the patterns call for you to turn something inside out, and then use the three-needle bind off on your live stitches, since this technique makes a nice finished seam. If you're not using the Magic Loop method (seriously, here's another benefit, just go learn it!), you will probably want to transfer your stitches to a circular needle of any size to turn your item inside out. It's much, much easier and much, much less terrifying to turn your monster inside out by threading the needle points of your circular needle through the bottom opening.

When you do turn your item inside out, you might notice that with the three-needle bind off, your yarn will be coming from the first stitch in the front, instead of the last stitch in the back like normal. No biggie! This is what it's supposed to look like for monsters, so just power on through.

Oh Holy Cupcakes, I Am Still Totally Stumped

Does a knitting technique or term still have you confused, even after my lovely guidelines? No worries; even knitting superheroes sometimes need to ask for help! The best places to go for help are either your local yarn shop or www.knittinghelp.com, a website that offers fantastic videos to help you every step of the way. Or, if you buy your supplies at a local yarn shop, they will be more than happy to help you out with any knitting questions you might have. They're not as good on the more, say, "What's the meaning of life?"–type questions, though. Trust me; I've asked. But you could ask them if there's a particular knitting reference book they recommend.

There you go. You've gotten through all the boring stuff. I now deem you officially ready to become a monster-knitting expert.

General Monster Finishing Guidelines

Putting your monster together brings his personality to life! The following are some helpful tips and tricks to make your monster come out just the way you are envisioning him.

Oh the Drudgery!
Weaving in the Ends

Unlike more traditional projects where it's very important to carefully weave in all of those little ends beautifully so they won't show through your project, toys allow for a little more wiggle room. I'll let you in on a little secret: even though I recommend the obligatory "weave in the ends" for all of the patterns, I don't ever weave in the ends. Your monsters are going to have a lovely inside filled with fluff that will hide the ends, so the most I usually do is just pull the ends to the inside of the project, and voilà! I'm done. All ends are hidden in the stuffing. I also generally leave a long tail when I cast on so I can use that tail to sew the body parts to the torso in the end, leaving me with even fewer ends to worry about. Then, to conceal that end once said limb is sewn to said torso, I pull the yarn through the body, right where I'm sewing the limb on, pull it out the opposite side of the body, and cut the yarn flush to the body. This instantly hides the tail every time!

The Art of Stuffing

Oh the art of stuffing, and yes it's truly an art! Stuffing your monster is what can make or break the final product. I think any stuffing technique or skill comes from practice. I have stuffed a lot of monsters and I swear that I learn something from each and every one.

I get asked all the time what type of stuffing I use. Honestly, I use the cheapest stuffing at the craft store. Seriously, when it's on sale I'll buy like 10 bags of the stuff and the craft store clerks always look at me like I have lobsters crawling out of my ears. (Especially when they ask what I'm going to use it for and I have to tell them that I make knitted monsters.) Anyway, I go through bags of this stuff and I can't really tell a difference between any of the brands, or materials, or anything. I just like to make sure I get the hypoallergenic stuffing. Purchase whatever stuffing you like best. Oh, and no, those bean pellet thingies (you know, what goes in Beanie Babies) are not a good idea for your monster. You could try wrapping them in fabric or something, and then dropping them in your monster, but I think the beans will still find their way out through the stitches and all over your floor. In my house this would mean that they would find their way directly into my pugs' mouths, which would lead to a lot of yelling and sticking my fingers in their mouths, but I digress.

As far as actually stuffing a monster, I like to think of myself as a sculpture artist whose medium is fluff. Make sure to take a lot of time for stuffing. Look at your monster from all sides: do you see a lump, valley, or hunchback? Smoosh the stuffing around to shape it, or add a little at a time until it looks right. If you keep stuffing and stuffing and it's just not looking right, it might be time to take all the stuffing out and start again. Make sure to use my samples for reference too—that's what they're there for! There is a lot of squashing and rolling and adding bits of fluff here and there when I work. I hope you, too, will become not just a fiber artist, but a stuffing artist like me.

Monster Surgery, or Sewing Everything Together

The easiest way to sew on monster ears, arms, legs, or feet is to flatten the open, cast-on edge of the appendage (basically think of folding the circle in half) and attach that edge to the body. This will make the limbs hang down to the sides, giving your critter a natural look—or, at least as natural as a stuffed, knitted monster can look.

Using straight pins, play around with the ear, arm, and leg placement. Refer to your monster's photo for placement, or be creative and place them where you think they should be. Once you're happy with how they look, go ahead and sew them down. Make sure to double-check that the second ear/arm/leg lines up with the first one before sewing it down.

For the actual attaching, I find using a whipstitch— essentially up, over, and around the cast-on edge of the ear or limb—works the best. Now, if only human surgery were this easy.

Button, Button, Who's Got the Belly Button?

Everyone has a belly button, right? So your monster needs a belly button too! Using a single strand of yarn and a tapestry needle, and referring to the photo for placement, make an X in the middle of your monster's belly as you stuff the body. Pull the ends to the inside and tie them in a small knot to make sure the belly button stays in place.

Put Your Best Face Forward

The face! This is where your monster's individual person-ality will come shining through. I think this is the tough-est part and probably where I spend the majority of my monster-making time. Yes, it can be challenging, but don't fret and lose sleep over your monster faces. I just talk to my half-finished monster to find out what's going to look right on him or her, and keep moving and remaking the facial features until I'm really happy with what I see. Eyes look weird? Try the next size up or down. Mouth just not feeling "right"? Cut a new one— it can seriously change the whole feel of the monster. Just take it slow and use my samples as a guide. And remember, if your monster looks really odd, it will just give him more character.

JEEPERS, CREEPERS, WHERE'D YOU GET THOSE SAFETY EYES?

I have included what size of safety eyes I used for each sample in this book. Now, as much as I would like to rule the world, this is only so you have a *general idea* about what is going to look best. Because every knitter knits very differently, I recommend you have a range of safety eyes in your knitting tool kit so that depending on how you've knit and stuffed your monster, you have additional options for eyes. I always try at least two sizes of eyes on each monster before deciding which one I like best, and I urge you to do the same. Safety eyes can be purchased at most craft stores, or online at www.6060.etsy.com. And, so you know what to buy, I use a general range of safety eyes from 7 mm to 18 mm.

Danger, Will Robinson! Safety

I like to use safety eyes for my monsters since they are quick and easy and give my toys a very consistent look. However, you must think of your monster's future owner before deciding to use safety eyes. Children under three years of age should never be given toys with things like safety eyes or ribbons that could possibly come off and be ingested. It's just as easy to embroider the eyes and other facial features as it is to use safety eyes and glued-on felt teeth. If you use straight pins to assemble your monster, make sure to use ones with colored heads so they are easy to see and remove; you don't want pins inadvertently left in the finished toy.

MONSTER MOUTHS

The monster mouth is one of my favorite parts. For the monsters with an actual mouth and one tooth (such as Claude, Geet, and Toothy Joe), it's pretty easy to cut a small rectangle tooth. I then glue down only the bottom edge of the tooth to make it more "3-D" when the monster is done.

For the spikey, toothy monster mouths, it takes a little more scissors ability. Using my monster's face as a gauge for width, I cut a rectangle of white felt, making sure to cut one edge super straight. Then, using extra sharp scissors, I cut up and down at an angle on the not-as-straight edge to create little pointed teeth. Be careful not to cut too far down between the teeth or the felt will want to pull apart as you're gluing it to the face. Be careful to not cut too shallow here either, or the teeth will look bulky. I know, I know, so picky! In the end it boils down to the fact that again, this is your monster and you can do whatever the heck you want with it. Just remember there's nothing that says you have to be perfect the first time, and you can recut the mouth as many times as you need to.

After your teeth look good to you, use your pins to position the teeth on the face where you want them to go and glue them down. Use some heavy books and stack them on your monster's face to secure the teeth until the glue dries. Cruel I know, but trust me, your monster will thank you for it when his teeth stay securely attached to his face.

Standard Yarn-Weight System

Yarn-Weight Symbol and Category Name	**1** Super Fine	**2** Fine	**3** Light	**4** Medium	**5** Bulky	**6** Super Bulky
Types of Yarn in Category	Sock, Fingering, Baby	Sport, Baby	DK, Light Worsted	Worsted, Afghan, Aran	Chunky, Craft, Rug	Bulky, Roving
Knit Gauge Range* in Stockinette Stitch to 4"	27 to 32 sts	23 to 26 sts	21 to 24 sts	16 to 20 sts	12 to 15 sts	6 to 11 sts
Recommended Needle in Metric Size Range	2.25 to 3.25 mm	3.25 to 3.75 mm	3.75 to 4.5 mm	4.5 to 5.5 mm	5.5 to 8 mm	8 mm and larger
Recommended Needle in U.S. Size Range	1 to 3	3 to 5	5 to 7	7 to 9	9 to 11	11 and larger

*These are guidelines only. The above reflect the most commonly used gauges and needle sizes for specific yarn categories.

Harold is a super easygoing monster who really likes to talk to plants. He likes to live in the planters of my house-plants, since he says that they keep him calm and collected. He works very, very hard at having a slow-paced, relaxing life, which he admits is not always easy to do.

Materials

It's easy to use any yarn-and-needle combination for this project. To find out more, see "What's the Deal with Gauge?" (page 5).

200–250 yards of yarn

1 set of double-pointed needles 2 or 3 sizes smaller than those recommended for yarn

Circular needle (36" or longer) in same size as dpns

Notions: tapestry needle, plastic safety eyes, white felt for teeth, fabric glue, stuffing, row counter (optional), stitch marker, straight pins (optional)

Samples

Green Harold

Finished size: 18" tall

2 skeins of Comfort Chunky from Berroco (50% superfine nylon, 50% superfine acrylic; 100 g/3.5 oz; 150 yds/138 m) in color 5740 **5**

U.S. size 9 (5.5 mm) needles

15 mm black safety eyes

Orange Harold

Finished size: 15" tall

1 skein of 220 Superwash from Cascade Yarns (100% superwash wool; 100 g/3.5 oz; 220 yds) in color 825 **3**

U.S. size 5 (3.75 mm) needles

12 mm black safety eyes

Body

Using the Magic Loop method (page 6), CO 60 sts and join, making sure not to twist sts. PM to indicate beg of rnd.

R1–R36: Knit all sts. *ben color*

R37: (K2tog, K28) twice. (58 sts)

R38: Knit all sts.

R39: (K27, K2tog) twice. (56 sts)

R40: Knit all sts.

R41: (K2tog, K26) twice. (54 sts)

R42: Knit all sts.

R43: (K25, K2tog) twice. (52 sts)

R44: Knit all sts.

R45: (K2tog, K24) twice. (50 sts)

R46: Knit all sts.

R47: (K23, K2tog) twice. (48 sts)

R48: Knit all sts.

R49: (K2tog, K22) twice. (46 sts)

R50: Knit all sts.

R51: (K21, K2tog) twice. (44 sts)

R52: (K2tog, K18, K2tog) twice. (40 sts)

R53: (K2tog, K16, K2tog) twice. (36 sts)

R54: (K2tog, K14, K2tog) twice. (32 sts)

Turn Harold inside out and work 3-needle BO on all sts. Turn Harold RS out and there you go—the start of a monster!

Base of Body

R1: Use dpns to PU 60 sts from CO edge of body (fig. 1). PM to indicate beg of rnd.

R2–R5: Knit all sts.

R6: (K3, K2tog) around. (48 sts)

R7: (K2, K2tog) around. (36 sts)

R8: (K1, K2tog) around. (24 sts)

Stop and stuff Harold. Sew on belly button and attach safety eyes now as well.

R9: (K2tog) around. (12 sts)

R10: (K2tog) around. (6 sts)

Cut yarn and using tapestry needle, thread through rem sts to close base.

Toes, Foot, and Leg (Make 2.)

Using dpns, evenly CO 6 sts and join, making sure not to twist sts.

R1: PM to indicate beg of rnd. K1f&b of all sts. (12 sts)

R2–R6: Knit all sts.

Cut your yarn and transfer toe sts to circular needle and make 2 more toes following above directions. For third toe, transfer sts to circular needle in middle of rnd so that working yarn becomes working yarn for foot (fig. 2).

FOOT

Using Magic Loop method, PM to indicate beg of rnd, and beg.

R1–R6: Knit all sts.

R7: (K2tog, K16) twice. (34 sts)

R8: Knit all sts.

R9: (K15, K2tog) twice. (32 sts)

R10: Knit all sts.

R11: (K2tog, K14) twice. (30 sts)

R12: Knit all sts.

R13: (K13, K2tog) twice. (28 sts)

R14: K3, switch to waste yarn (in different color than working yarn) and knit across next 8 sts. Purl back across these same 8 sts, still using waste yarn. (This will become the leg.) Now switch back to working yarn and knit all sts to end of rnd.

(Fig. 1)

Blue stitches representing picked-up stitches

(Fig. 2)

Toes on circular needle

R15: (K2tog, K10, K2tog) twice. (24 sts)

R16: Knit all sts.

R17: (K2tog, K8, K2tog) twice. (20 sts)

R18: Knit all sts.

R19: (K2tog, K6, K2tog) twice. (16 sts)

Cut yarn and with tapestry needle, use Kitchener st to close back of foot.

LEG

To knit leg, release 16 sts held on waste yarn from R14 and transfer them to dpns (fig. 3). PM to indicate beg of rnd.

R1: Knit all sts, making sure to PU 1 additional st per side of leg opening. (18 sts)

R2: (K2tog, K4) three times. (15 sts) Stop and stuff foot and toes now.

R3–R22: Knit all sts.

R23: BO all sts.

Arm and Thumb

(Make 2.)

ARM

Using dpns, evenly CO 12 sts and join, making sure not to twist sts. PM to indicate beg of rnd.

R1–R30: Knit all sts.

R31: (K2tog, K4) twice. (10 sts)

R32: Knit all sts.

R33: (K1f&b, K4) twice. (12 sts)

R34: (K5, K1f&b) twice. (14 sts)

R35 and R36: Knit all sts.

R37: K6, K1f&b, knit to end. (15 sts)

R38: Knit all sts.

R39: K8, K1f&b, knit to end. (16 sts)

R40: Knit all sts.

R41: K6, place next 4 sts on waste yarn and cont knitting across gap to end of rnd.

R42–R48: Knit all sts.

R49: (K2tog, K4) twice. (10 sts)

Cut yarn and with tapestry needle, use Kitchener st to close top of hand.

THUMB

Place 4 live sts on dpns and PU 4 more sts around thumb opening (8 sts total). PM to indicate beg of rnd.

R1–R4: Knit all sts.

R5: (K2tog) all sts. (4 sts)

Cut yarn and using tapestry needle, thread through rem sts to close thumb.

Finishing

Are you ready to bring your monster to life? Turn to "General Monster Finishing Guidelines" on page 10 for detailed finishing directions.

That's it! You've created a monster! Wasn't it easy to make such an easygoing guy? Do keep your eye on Harold, though. He tends to talk to those houseplants a little too much sometimes and he might need to be directed away from the plants and toward things that actually respond to him.

(Fig. 3)

Releasing held stitches from round 14 of foot

Baldwin
the Bathroom Monster

Baldwin is one of the sweetest monsters I know, but he's not super bright. Baldwin is a bathroom monster, living under my bathroom sink. One of his favorite activities is unrolling the toilet paper when no one is watching, so that no matter how often you change it, it seems like it always needs replacing. His other hobbies include draining shampoo down the sink (so that you always seem to have less shampoo than conditioner), mashing the toothpaste tube in the middle, and rearranging the medicine cabinet in the middle of the night. He's also responsible for the toothpaste spray marks you might find on your mirror.

17

Materials

It's easy to use any yarn-and-needle combination for this project. To find out more, see "What's the Deal with Gauge?" (page 5).

100–150 yards of yarn

1 set of double-pointed needles 2 or 3 sizes smaller than those recommended for yarn

Circular needle (36" or longer) in same size as dpns

Notions: tapestry needle, plastic safety eyes, white felt for teeth, fabric glue, stuffing, row counter (optional), stitch marker, straight pins (optional)

Samples

Green Baldwin

Finished size: 17" tall

4 skeins of Outer from Spud and Chloë (65% superwash wool, 35% organic cotton; 100 g; 60 yds/55 m) in color 7204 (**6**)

U.S. size 11 (8 mm) needles

18 mm black safety eyes

Orange Baldwin

Finished size: 8" tall

1 skein of Fisherman from Lorna's Laces (100% wool; 500 yds) in color 508 Winona (**4**)

U.S. size 6 (4 mm) needles

12 mm black safety eyes

Leg (Make 2.)

Using dpns, evenly CO 6 sts and join, making sure not to twist sts. PM to indicate beg of rnd.

R1: K1f&b in all sts. (12 sts)

R2: K1f&b in all sts. (24 sts)

R3–R12: Knit all sts.

At the end of rnd 12, backward-loop CO 12 sts and cut yarn. (36 sts)

Following "The Legs to Body Situation" (page 8), transfer leg sts to circular needle as follows. For first leg, put 12 sts on front needle and 24 sts (12 leg plus 12 CO) on back needle. For second leg, again make sure to cut yarn, and put 24 sts (12 leg plus 12 CO) on front needle and 12 sts on back needle. You'll have 72 total sts, and new beg of rnd in middle of Baldwin's second leg.

Body

Using Magic Loop method (page 6), PM to indicate beg of rnd, and beg.

R1–R6: Knit all sts.

R7: (K2tog, K34) twice. (70 sts)

R8 and R9: Knit all sts.

R10: (K33, K2tog) twice. (68 sts)

R11 and R12: Knit all sts.

R13: (K2tog, K32) twice. (66 sts)

R14 and R15: Knit all sts.

R16: (K31, K2tog) twice. (64 sts)

R17 and R18: Knit all sts.

R19: (K2tog, K30) twice. (62 sts)

R20 and R21: Knit all sts.

R22: (K29, K2tog) twice. (60 sts)

R23 and R24: Knit all sts.

R25: (K2tog, K28) twice. (58 sts)

R26 and R27: Knit all sts.

R28: (K27, K2tog) twice. (56 sts)

R29 and R30: Knit all sts.

R31: (K2tog, K26) twice. (54 sts)

R32 and R33: Knit all sts.

R34: (K25, K2tog) twice. (52 sts)

R35 and R36: Knit all sts.

R37: (K2tog, K24) twice. (50 sts)

R38 and R39: Knit all sts.

R40: (K23, K2tog) twice. (48 sts)

R41 and R42: Knit all sts.

R43: (K2tog, K22) twice. (46 sts)

R44 and R45: Knit all sts.

R46: (K21, K2tog) twice. (44 sts)

R47 and R48: Knit all sts.

R49: (K2tog, K20) twice. (42 sts)

R50 and R51: Knit all sts.

R52: (K19, K2tog) twice. (40 sts)

R53 and R54: Knit all sts.

R55: (K2tog, K16, K2tog) twice. (36 sts)

Turn Baldwin inside out and work 3-needle BO on all sts. Turn Baldwin RS out and admire your amazing monster handiwork!

Arm (Make 2.)

Using dpns, evenly CO 9 sts and join, making sure not to twist sts. PM to indicate beg of rnd.

R1–R30: Knit all sts.

R31: K1f&b in first 6 sts of rnd, knit to end. (15 sts)

R32–R39: Knit all sts.

R40: K2tog around, end K1. (8 sts)

Cut yarn and using tapestry needle, thread through rem sts to close hand.

Finishing

Are you ready to bring your monster to life? Turn to "General Monster Finishing Guidelines" on page 10 for detailed finishing directions. Make sure to attach Baldwin's arm with the rounded, "hand" side of his arm facing in toward his body.

Tah-dah! You made a monster! Try as you might, Baldwin will find his way into your bathroom and test your patience with his creative bathroom antics. It can get to be rather annoying, but luckily Baldwin does seem easily entertained. It might behoove you to leave some jacks, puzzles, or coloring books under the sink for him so he'll leave your toiletries alone.

Angus
the Attic Monster

Angus's favorite place to be is in my attic, so he happily lives there most of the time. He loves it up there since he can get a good view of everything going on, plus he really likes the pigeons that live near the roof and the eaves. Angus thinks pigeons are really great listeners and he'll talk to them for hours on end, or until they get bored and fly away. The only thing Angus doesn't like about living in the attic is that people tend to store the oddest things up there. For the life of him he can't figure out what the long flat boards with weird hooky things and the letters "knit-5" on them are. Luckily the pigeons are generally happy to talk him through his confusions.

Materials

It's easy to use any yarn-and-needle combination for this project. To find out more, see "What's the Deal with Gauge?" (page 5).

180–230 yards of yarn

1 set of double-pointed needles 2 or 3 sizes smaller than those recommended for yarn

Notions: tapestry needle, plastic safety eyes, white felt for teeth, fabric glue, stuffing, row counter (optional), stitch marker, straight pins (optional)

Samples

Green Angus
Finished size: 18" tall

2 skeins of Cash Vero from Cascade Yarns (55% merino extra fine wool, 33% microfiber acrylic, 12% cashmere; 50 g; 98 yds) in color 045 [4]

U.S. size 5 (3.75 mm) needles

9 mm black safety eyes

Red Angus
Finished size: 22" tall

2 skeins of Shepherd Bulky from Lorna's Laces (100% superwash wool; 140 yds) in color 50ns Poppy [5]

U.S. size 9 (5.5 mm) needles

12 mm black safety eyes

Body

Using dpns, evenly CO 6 sts and join, making sure not to twist sts. PM to indicate beg of rnd.

R1: K1f&b all sts. (12 sts)

R2: Knit all sts.

R3: K1f&b all sts. (24 sts)

R4: Knit all sts.

R5: (K1f&b, K1) around. (36 sts)

R6: Knit all sts.

R7: (K1f&b, K2) around. (48 sts)

R8: Knit all sts.

R9: (K1f&b, K3) around. (60 sts)

R10: Knit all sts.

R11: (K1f&b, K4) around. (72 sts)

R12–R26: Knit all sts.

R27: (K2tog, K4) around. (60 sts)

R28: Knit all sts.

R29: (K2tog, K3) around. (48 sts)

R30: Knit all sts.

R31: (K2tog, K2) around. (36 sts)

R32: Knit all sts.

R33: (K2tog, K1) around. (24 sts)

R34: Knit all sts.

Stop, add belly button, and stuff body.

R35: K2tog around. (12 sts)

R36: Knit all sts.

R37: K1f&b all sts. (24 sts)

R38: Knit all sts.

R39: (K1f&b, K1) around. (36 sts)

R40: Knit all sts.

R41: (K1f&b, K2) around. (48 sts)

R42–R53: Knit all sts.

R54: (K2tog, K2) around. (36 sts)

R55: Knit all sts.

R56: (K2tog, K1) around (24 sts)

R57: Knit all sts.

Stop again and stuff head and neck. Make sure to attach safety eyes now as well, lining them up so they are centered over belly button.

R58: K2tog around. (12 sts)

R59: Knit all sts.

R60: K2tog. (6 sts)

R61–R74: Switch to 2 dpns and knit all sts as an I-cord.

Cut yarn and using tapestry needle, thread through rem sts to close head. Tie I-cord into knot, snugging it up against the head.

Leg (Make 2.)

Using dpns, evenly CO 14 sts, join, making sure not to twist sts. PM to indicate beg of rnd.

R1-R55: Knit all sts.

Place first 6 sts of rnd on 1 needle and next 8 sts on second needle.

Work heel on last 8 sts.

R1: Sl1p, purl to end, turn.

R2: Sl1k, knit to end, turn.

R3: Sl1p, purl to end, turn.

R4: Sl1k, knit to end, turn.

R5: Sl1p, purl to end, turn.

R6: Sl1k, knit to end, turn.

R7: Sl1p, purl to end, turn.

Beg foot

R1: PM, this will become new beg of rnd. Knit across heel sts once more. Using new dpn, PU 5 sts from left side of heel flap, knit across half of held instep sts with same needle, knit across rest of held instep sts on third dpn, and PU 5 sts from right side of heel flap with same needle (fig. 1). (24 sts)

R2: Knit all sts.

R3: (K8, K2tog, K2tog) twice. (20 sts)

R4: Knit all sts.

R5: (K8, K2tog) twice. (18 sts)

R6–R16: Knit all sts.

R17: (K7, K2tog) around. (16 sts)

Cut yarn and with tapestry needle, use Kitchener st to close foot.

Picking up stitches on heel flap

Arm and Thumb
(Make 2.)

ARM

Using dpns, evenly CO 12 sts and join, making sure not to twist sts. PM to indicate beg of rnd.

R1–R40: Knit all sts.

R41: K2tog around. (6 sts)

R42: Knit all sts.

R43: K1f&b around. (12 sts)

R44: Knit all sts.

R45: (K1f&b, K1) around. (18 sts)

R46: Knit all sts.

R47: K7, place next 4 sts on waste yarn, knit across gap, and knit to end. (14 sts)

R48–R56: Knit all sts.

R57: (K2tog, K5) twice. (12 sts)

Cut yarn and with tapestry needle, use Kitchener st to close hand.

THUMB

Move held sts back to needles and PU 5 additional sts around thumb-hole. You will have 9 total sts. PM to indicate beg of rnd.

R1–R6: Knit all sts.

Cut yarn and using tapestry needle, thread through rem sts to close thumb.

Finishing

Are you ready to bring your monster to life? Turn to "General Monster Finishing Guidelines" on page 10 for detailed finishing directions.

Awesome! You've made an attic monster. Now let him go do his thing and hang out with the pigeons in your attic. Even if they pretend to not enjoy talking to Angus—some might even fly away from boredom—the pigeons really are as happy to talk to Angus as he is to them. I like win-win situations like this, don't you? Oh, but you might want to explain those skis to him, though he still might not understand them entirely.

Lurleen
the Laundry Monster

Lurleen lives by my washer and dryer. She really likes tormenting humans while they do laundry, possibly since most folks are already cranky when they do chores like laundry. Lurleen is responsible for stunts like throwing a red sock in with your white clothes, creating a pink-hued load; or moving laundry mid-cycle so no matter what you do the load is unbalanced; or putting pure wool in a warm wash cycle and felting your favorite sweater. She also likes to throw laundry powder on the floor and add pieces of paper to loads so you get confetti in your clothes.

Materials

It's easy to use any yarn-and-needle combination for this project. To find out more, see "What's the Deal with Gauge?" (page 5).

100–140 yards of yarn in main color (MC)
20–30 yards of yarn in contrasting color (CC)
1 set of double-pointed needles 2 or 3 sizes smaller than those recommended for yarn
Notions: tapestry needle, plastic safety eyes, white felt for teeth, fabric glue, stuffing, row counter (optional), stitch marker, straight pins (optional)

Samples

Pink-and-Yellow Lurleen
Finished size: 9" tall

MC 1 skein of Cascade 220 Wool from Cascade Yarns (100% Peruvian Highland wool; 100 g/3.5 oz; 220 yds/200 m) in color 7804 (**4**)
CC 1 skein of Cascade 220 Heathers from Cascade Yarns (100% Merino wool; 100 g/3.5 oz; 220 yds) in color 2439
U.S. size 5 (3.75 mm) needles
9 mm black safety eyes

Blue-and-Red Lurleen
Finished size: 13" tall

MC 2 skeins of Baby Alpaca Grande from Plymouth Yarn Company (100% baby alpaca; 100g; 110 yds) in color 3317 (**5**)
CC 1 skein of Baby Alpaca Grande from Plymouth Yarn Company in color 2050
U.S. size 9 (5.5 mm) needles
12 mm black safety eyes

Body

Using dpns, evenly CO 6 sts in MC and join, making sure not to twist sts. PM to indicate beg of rnd.

R1: K1f&b all sts. (12 sts)

R2: K1f&b all sts. (24 sts)

R3: Knit all sts.

R4: (K1f&b, K1) around. (36 sts)

R5: Knit all sts.

R6: (K1f&b, K2) around. (48 sts)

R7–R30: Knit all sts.

R31: (K2tog, K20, K2tog) twice. (44 sts)

R32 and R33: Knit all sts.

R34: (K2tog, K18, K2tog) twice. (40 sts)

R35 and R36: Knit all sts.

R37: (K2tog, K16, K2tog) twice. (36 sts)

R38 and R39: Knit all sts.

R40: (K2tog, K14, K2tog) twice. (32 sts)

R41 and R42: Knit all sts.

R43: (K2tog, K12, K2tog) twice. (28 sts)

R44 and R45: Knit all sts.

R46: (K2tog, K10, K2tog) twice. (24 sts)

R47 and R48: Knit all sts.

R49: (K2tog, K8, K2tog) twice. (20 sts)

Stop and stuff body. Make sure to add belly button now as well!

R50: (K2tog, K6, K2tog) twice. (16 sts)

R51 and R52: Knit all sts.

R53: (K1f&b, K6, K1f&b) twice. (20 sts)

R54: (K1f&b, K8, K1f&b) twice. (24 sts)

R55: (K1f&b, K10, K1f&b) twice. (28 sts)

R56: (K1f&b, K12, K1f&b) twice. (32 sts)

R57–R70: Knit all sts.

R71: (K2tog, K12, K2tog) twice. (28 sts)

R72: (K2tog, K10, K2tog) twice. (24 sts)

R73: (K2tog, K8, K2tog) twice. (20 sts)

R74: (K2tog, K6, K2tog) twice. (16 sts)

Stop again and stuff head and neck. Make sure to attach safety eyes now as well, lining them up so they're centered over belly button.

R75: (K2tog, K4, K2tog) twice. (12 sts)

Cut yarn and with tapestry needle, use Kitchener st to close head. Now you've got a bowling-pin-shaped monster body. Pretty cool, huh?

Arm (Make 2.)

Using dpns, evenly CO 10 sts in MC and join, making sure not to twist sts. PM to indicate beg of rnd.

R1–R28: Knit all sts.

R29: K1f&b of first 5 sts of rnd, K5. (15 sts)

R30–R38: Knit all sts.

R39: K2tog around, end K1. (8 sts)

Cut yarn and using tapestry needle, thread through rem sts to close hand.

Foot (Make 2.)

Using dpns, evenly CO 10 sts in MC and join, making sure not to twist sts. PM to indicate beg of rnd.

R1: Knit all sts.

R2: (K1f&b, K4) twice. (12 sts)

R3: Knit all sts.

R4: (K5, K1f&b) twice. (14 sts)

R5: Knit all sts.

R6: (K1f&b, K6) twice. (16 sts)

R7: Knit all sts.

R8: (K7, K1f&b) twice. (18 sts)

R9–R15: Knit all sts.

R16: (K2tog, K7) twice. (16 sts)

R17: Knit all sts.

R18: (K6, K2tog) twice. (14 sts)

R19: Knit all sts.

R20: K2tog around (7 sts).

Cut yarn and using tapestry needle, thread through rem sts to close foot.

Small Spot (Make 2.)

Using dpns, evenly CO 4 sts in CC and join, making sure not to twist sts. PM to indicate beg of rnd.

R1: K1f&b all sts. (8 sts)

R2: K1f&b all sts. (16 sts)

R3: Knit all sts.

R4: BO all sts purlwise.

Large Spot

Using dpns, evenly CO 4 sts in CC and join, making sure not to twist sts. PM to indicate beg of rnd.

R1: K1f&b all sts. (8 sts)

R2: K1f&b all sts. (16 sts)

R3: (K1, K1f&b) around. (24 sts)

R4: Knit all sts.

R5: BO all sts purlwise.

Finishing

Are you ready to bring your monster to life? Turn to "General Monster Finishing Guidelines" on page 10 for detailed finishing directions. Make sure to attach Lurleen's arm with the rounded, "hand" side of her arm facing in toward her body.

For the spots, I sew them down so that the wrong (purl) side is up. I play around with placement using my straight pins and position them slightly under one arm and around to the back. You put them wherever you think they look best and once you're happy, sew around them to secure them to the body.

Done and done. You've now got a great-looking laundry monster! Try as you may to thwart her, Lurleen will still find her way to your washing machine to play her annoying tricks on you. You might try introducing Lurleen to felting, though; it seems like it would be a hobby that's right up her alley since it involves the washer!

Geet
the Garage Monster

Geet is a very odd little monster that lives in my garage. He likes to hang out in there, playing around with all the bits and pieces he finds. Geet is also very fond of being mischievous: he will sneak rides in my car so that he can run around parking lots with a tiny hammer and chisel and leave dings in people's car doors. I know there are many theories out there about how these little dings happen—reckless drivers, gnomes, pebbles, and more—but in fact it's a door-dinging monster like Geet leaving his calling card. Luckily he will generally not damage the car he sneaks around in, but I can't promise anything.

Materials

It's easy to use any yarn-and-needle combination for this project. To find out more, see "What's the Deal with Gauge?" (page 5).

140–190 yards of yarn in main color (MC)

20–40 yards of yarn in contrasting color (CC)

1 set of double-pointed needles 2 or 3 sizes smaller than those recommended for yarn

Circular needle (36" or longer) in same size as dpns

Notions: tapestry needle, plastic safety eyes, white felt for teeth, fabric glue, stuffing, row counter (optional), stitch marker, straight pins (optional)

Samples

Green-and-Aqua Geet
Finished size: 16" tall

MC 1 skein of Comfort from Berroco (50% super fine nylon, 50% super fine acrylic; 100 g/3.5 oz; 210 yds/193 m) in color 9740 **4**

CC 1 skein of Comfort from Berroco in color 9733

U.S. size 7 (4.5 mm) needles

12 mm black safety eyes

Yellow-and-Pink Geet
Finished size: 21" tall

MC 2 skeins of Baby Alpaca Grande from Plymouth Yarn Company (100% baby alpaca; 100 g; 110 yds) in color 1709 **5**

CC 1 skein of Baby Alpaca Grande from Plymouth Yarn Company in color 69

U.S. size 5 (3.75 mm) needles

15 mm black safety eyes

Body and Base

BODY

Using the Magic Loop method (page 6), CO 40 sts in MC and join, making sure not to twist sts. PM to indicate beg of rnd.

R1–R7: Knit all sts.

R8: (K1f&b, K19) twice. (42 sts)

R9–R15: Knit all sts.

R16: (K20, K1f&b) twice. (44 sts)

R17–R23: Knit all sts.

R24: (K1f&b, K21) twice. (46 sts)

R25–R31: Knit all sts.

R32: (K22, K1f&b) twice. (48 sts)

R33–R37: Knit all sts.

R38: BO first 24 sts of rnd, knit to end of rnd.

R39: PU 24 sts along BO edge through both loops, knit to end of rnd. The last 2 rnds create a line that will become Geet's mouth.

R40–R54: Knit all sts.

R55: (K2tog, K20, K2tog) twice. (44 sts)

R56: (K2tog, K18, K2tog) twice. (40 sts)

R57: (K2tog, K16, K2tog) twice. (36 sts)

Turn Geet inside out and work 3-needle BO on all sts. Turn Geet RS out and there you go: the start of a monster!

BASE OF BODY

Work base in MC.

R1: Use dpns to PU 40 sts from CO edge of body (fig. 1). PM to indicate beg of rnd.

R2–R5: Knit all sts.

R6: (K2, K2tog) around. (30 sts)

R7: (K1, K2tog) around. (20 sts)

Stop and stuff Geet. Sew on belly button and attach plastic safety eyes now as well.

R8: (K2tog) around. (10 sts)

R9: (K2tog) around. (5 sts)

Cut yarn and using tapestry needle, thread through rem sts to close base.

Ear (Make 2.)

Using dpns, evenly CO 14 sts in CC and join, making sure not to twist sts. PM to indicate beg of rnd.

R1: Knit all sts.

R2: (K1f&b, K6) twice. (16 sts)

R3: Knit all sts.

R4: (K7, K1f&b) twice. (18 sts)

R5–R12: Knit all sts.

R13: (K2tog, K5, K2tog) twice. (14 sts)

R14: (K2tog, K3, K2tog) twice. (10 sts)

R15: (K2tog) around. (5 sts)

Cut yarn and using tapestry needle, thread through rem sts to close ear.

(Fig. 1)

Blue stitches representing picked-up stitches

Arm (Make 2.)

Using dpns, evenly CO 12 sts in MC and join, making sure not to twist sts. PM to indicate beg of rnd.

R1–R24: Knit all sts.

R25: K1f&b of first 6 sts, knit to end. (18 sts)

R26–R33: Knit all sts.

R34: (K1, K2tog) around. (12 sts)

R35: Knit all sts.

R36: K2tog around. (6 sts)

Cut yarn and using tapestry needle, thread through rem sts to close hand.

Leg (Make 2.)

Using dpns, evenly CO 12 sts in MC and join, making sure not to twist sts. PM to indicate beg of rnd.

R1–R32: Knit all sts.

Place first 6 sts of rnd on 1 needle and second 6 sts on second needle.

Work heel with last 6 sts.

R1: Sl1p, purl to end, turn.

R2: Sl1k, knit to end, turn.

R3: Sl1p, purl to end, turn.

R4: Sl1k, knit to end, turn.

R5: Sl1p, purl to end, turn.

R6: Sl1k, knit to end, turn.

R7: Sl1p, purl to end, turn.

Beg foot

R1: PM, this will become new beg of rnd. Knit across heel sts once more. Using new dpn, PU 5 sts from left side of heel flap, knit across half of held instep sts with same needle, knit across rest of held instep sts on third dpn, and PU 5 sts from RS of heel flap with same needle (fig. 2). (22 sts)

R2: Knit all sts.

R3: (K7, K2tog, K2tog) twice. (18 sts)

R4: Knit all sts.

R5: (K7, K2tog) twice. (16 sts)

R6–R17: Knit all sts.

R18: (K6, K2tog) around. (14 sts)

Cut yarn and with tapestry needle, use Kitchener st to close foot.

Finishing

Are you ready to bring your monster to life? Turn to "General Monster Finishing Guidelines" on page 10 for detailed finishing directions.

Eureka! A knitted monster! I know Geet's habits might seem a little bit destructive, so you might want to dissuade him from going to the garage as much as possible. Putting out a puzzle or playing a board game with him might help, but don't be surprised if you do find him in your car eventually.

(Fig. 2)

Picking up stitches on heel flap

Charlie
the Ceiling Monster

Charlie is a little monster who likes to hop around the house without ever touching the floor. It seems he thinks the floor is made of lava, so he tends to sleep on the blades of a ceiling fan or in larger light fixtures to protect himself. He's also sneaky and does things like hopping on the corners of picture frames to make them crooked, or unscrewing light bulbs so people think that they have a burned-out light. Normally he stays out of sight, but sometimes if you watch really carefully you can see his long legs dangling from a shelf or on top of the refrigerator.

Materials

It's easy to use any yarn-and-needle combination for this project. To find out more, see "What's the Deal with Gauge?" (page 5).

70–120 yards of yarn in main color (MC)

30–80 yards of yarn in contrasting color (CC)

1 set of double-pointed needles 2 or 3 sizes smaller than those recommended for yarn

Circular needle (36" or longer) in same size as dpns

Notions: tapestry needle, plastic safety eyes, white felt for teeth, fabric glue, stuffing, row counter (optional), stitch marker, straight pins (optional)

Samples

Orange-and-Aqua Charlie

Finished size: 12" tall

MC 1 skein of Pure Pima from Berroco (100% pima cotton; 50 g/1.75 oz; 115 yds/106 m) in color 2236 (3)

CC 1 skein of Pure Pima from Berroco in color 2241

U.S. size 4 (3.5 mm) needles

9 mm black safety eyes

Pink-and-Green Charlie

Finished size: 13" tall

MC 1 skein of Sweater from Spud and Chloë (55% superwash wool, 45% organic cotton; 100 g; 160 yds/146 m) in color 7512 (4)

CC 1 skein of Sweater from Spud and Chloë in color 7502

U.S. size 7 (4.5 mm) needles

12 mm black safety eyes

Body and Base

BODY

Using the Magic Loop method (page 6), CO 36 sts in MC and join, making sure not to twist sts. PM to indicate beg or rnd.

R1–R24: Knit all sts.

R25: (K2tog, K16) twice. (34 sts)

R26: Knit all sts.

R27: (K15, K2tog) twice. (32 sts)

R28: Knit all sts.

R29: (K2tog, K14) twice. (30 sts)

R30: Knit all sts.

R31: (K13, K2tog) twice. (28 sts)

R32: Knit all sts.

R33: (K2tog, K12) twice. (26 sts)

R34: Knit all sts.

R35: (K11, K2tog) twice. (24 sts)

R36: (K2tog, K8, K2tog) twice. (20 sts)

R37: (K2tog, K6, K2tog) twice. (16 sts)

R38: (K2tog, K4, K2tog) twice. (12 sts)

Turn Charlie inside out and work 3-needle BO on all sts. Turn Charlie RS out and check out the mini monster!

BASE OF BODY

Work base in MC.

R1: Use dpns to PU 36 sts from CO edge of body (fig. 1). PM to indicate beg of rnd.

R2–R4: Knit all sts.

R5: (K2tog, K2) around. (27 sts)

R6: (K2tog. K1) around. (18 sts)

Stop and stuff Charlie. Sew on belly button and attach plastic safety eyes now as well.

R7: (K2tog) around. (9 sts)

Cut yarn and using tapestry needle, thread through rem sts to close base.

Arm (Make 2.)

Using dpns, evenly CO 12 sts in MC and join, making sure not to twist sts. PM to indicate beg of rnd.

R1–R14: Knit all sts.

R15: K2tog around. (6 sts)

Cut yarn and using tapestry needle, thread through rem sts to close hand.

Leg (Make 2.)

Using dpns, evenly CO 12 sts in CC and join, making sure not to twist sts. PM to indicate beg of rnd.

R1–R3: Knit all sts in CC.

R4–R42: Knit all sts in 2 rnds MC, 2 rnds CC.

Place first 4 sts on 1 needle and next 8 sts on second needle.

Cont with CC and work heel with last 8 sts.

R1: Sl1p, purl to end, turn.

R2: Sl1k, knit to end, turn.

R3: Sl1p, purl to end, turn.

R4: Sl1k, knit to end, turn.

R5: Sl1p, purl to end, turn.

Beg foot

R1: PM, this will become new beg of rnd. Knit across heel sts once more. Using new dpn, PU 3 sts from left side of heel flap, knit across half of held instep sts with same needle, knit across rest of held instep sts on third dpn, and PU 3 sts from right side of heel flap with same needle (fig. 2). (18 sts)

R2: Knit all sts.

R3: K6, K2tog, K2tog, K4, K2tog, K2tog. (14 sts)

R4: Knit all sts.

R5: (K5, K2tog) twice. (12 sts)

R6–R13: Knit all sts.

R14: (K4, K2tog) twice. (10 sts)

Cut yarn and using tapestry needle, use Kitchener st to close foot.

Finishing

Are you ready to bring your monster to life? Turn to "General Monster Finishing Guidelines" on page 10 for detailed finishing directions.

Yeah! A petite finished monster! Don't be too surprised if you don't see much of Charlie after this point; he really likes to stay hidden. If you do want to encourage him, it's best to have a strategic path of items—like pots, pans, plants, and books—on the floor so that he has things to hop on.

(Fig. 1)

Blue stitches representing picked-up stitches

(Fig. 2)

Picking up stitches on heel flap

Dot the Dress-Up Box Monster

Dot is a complete glamour monster and loves everything having to do with fashion and style. You can generally find her in the dress-up box, playing with the fabrics and clothes. Dot idolizes all of the glamour greats: Audrey Hepburn, Marilyn Monroe, Sophia Loren, Rita Hayworth, Coco Chanel, and many more. In fact, if you can't find her playing dress up, she's probably watching an old Hollywood glam movie featuring one of her fashion favorites!

35

Materials

It's easy to use any yarn-and-needle combination for this project. To find out more, see "What's the Deal with Gauge?" (page 5).

170–220 yards of yarn in main color (MC)

40–80 yards of yarn in contrasting color (CC)

1 set of double-pointed needles 2 or 3 sizes smaller than those recommended for yarn

Circular needle (36" or longer) in same size as dpns

Notions: tapestry needle, plastic safety eyes, white felt for teeth, fabric glue, stuffing, row counter (optional), stitch marker, straight pins (optional)

Samples

Pink-and-Red Dot

Finished size: 14" tall

MC 2 skeins of Pastaza from Cascade Yarns (50% llama, 50% wool; 100 g/3.5 oz; 132 yds) in color 310 (**4**)

CC 1 skein of Pastaza from Cascade Yarns in color 309

U.S. size 7 (4.5 mm) needles

15 mm black safety eyes

Green-and-Aqua Dot

Finished size: 15" tall

MC 2 skeins of Comfort Chunky from Berroco (50% super fine nylon, 50% super fine acrylic; 100 g/3.5 oz; 150 yds/138 m) in color 5740 (**5**)

CC 1 skein of Comfort Chunky from Berroco in color 5725

U.S. size 9 (5.5 mm) needles

15 mm black safety eyes

Leg (Make 2.)

Using dpns, evenly CO 6 sts in MC and join, making sure not to twist sts. PM to indicate beg or rnd.

R1: K1f&b all sts. (12 sts)

R2: K1f&b all sts. (24 sts)

R3: (K1f&b, K3) around. (30 sts)

R4–R10: Knit all sts.

At end of rnd 10, backward-loop CO 12 sts and cut yarn. (42 sts)

Following instructions in "The Legs to Body Situation" (page 8), transfer leg sts to circular needle as follows. For first leg, put 15 sts on front needle and 27 sts (15 leg plus 12 CO) on back needle. For second leg, again make sure to cut yarn, and put 27 sts (15 leg plus 12 CO) on front needle and 15 sts on back needle. You will have 84 total sts, and new beg of rnd in middle of Dot's second leg.

Body

Using Magic Loop method (page 6), PM to indicate beg of rnd and beg.

R1–R15: Knit all sts.

R16: (K2tog, K40) twice. (82 sts)

R17 and R18: Knit all sts.

R19: (K39, K2tog) twice. (80 sts)

R20 and R21: Knit all sts.

R22: (K2tog, K38) twice. (78 sts)

R23 and R24: Knit all sts.

R25: (K37, K2tog) twice. (76 sts)

R26 and R27: Knit all sts.

R28: (K2tog, K36) twice. (74 sts)

R29 and R30: Knit all sts.

R31: (K35, K2tog) twice. (72 sts)

R32 and R33: Knit all sts.

R34: (K2tog, K34) twice. (70 sts)

R35 and R36: Knit all sts.

R37: (K33, K2tog) twice. (68 sts)

R38 and R39: Knit all sts.

R40: (K2tog, K32) twice. (66 sts)

R41 and R42: Knit all sts.

R43: (K31, K2tog) twice. (64 sts)

R44 and R45: Knit all sts.

R46: (K2tog, K30) twice. (62 sts)

R47 and R48: Knit all sts.

R49: (K29, K2tog) twice. (60 sts)

R50 and R51: Knit all sts.

R52: (K2tog, K28) twice. (58 sts)

R53 and R54: Knit all sts.

R55: (K27, K2tog) twice. (56 sts)

R56 and R57: Knit all sts.

R58: (K2tog, K26) twice. (54 sts)

R59 and R60: Knit all sts.

R61: (K25, K2tog) twice. (52 sts)

R62: (K2tog, K22, K2tog) twice. (48 sts)

R63: (K2tog, K20, K2tog) twice. (44 sts)

R64: (K2tog, K18, K2tog) twice. (40 sts)

R65: (K2tog, K16, K2tog) twice. (36 sts)

Turn Dot inside out and work 3-needle BO on all sts. Turn Dot RS out and keep up the great monster knitting!

Arm (Make 2.)

Using dpns, evenly CO 18 sts in MC and join, making sure not to twist sts. PM to indicate beg of rnd.

R1–R28: Knit all sts.

R29: K2tog around. (9 sts)

Cut yarn and using tapestry needle, thread through rem sts to close hand.

Ear (Make 2.)

Using dpns, evenly CO 24 sts in CC and join, making sure not to twist sts. PM to indicate beg of rnd.

R1: Knit all sts.

R2: (K2tog, K10) twice. (22 sts)

R3: Knit all sts.

R4: (K9, K2tog) twice. (20 sts)

R5: Knit all sts.

R6: (K2tog, K8) twice. (18 sts)

R7: Knit all sts.

R8: (K7, K2tog) twice. (16 sts)

R9: Knit all sts.

R10: (K2tog, K6) twice. (14 sts)

R11: Knit all sts.

R12: (K5, K2tog) twice. (12 sts)

R13: Knit all sts.

R14: (K2tog, K4) twice. (10 sts)

R15: Knit all sts.

R16: K2tog around. (5 sts)

Cut yarn and using tapestry needle, thread through rem sts to close ear.

Eye Patch

Using dpns, evenly CO 6 sts in CC and join, making sure not to twist sts. PM to indicate beg of rnd.

R1: K1f&b all sts. (12 sts)

R2: (K1, K1f&b) around. (18 sts)

R3: (K2, K1f&b) around. (24 sts)

R4: Knit all sts.

R5: BO all sts pw.

Finishing

Are you ready to bring your monster to life? Turn to "General Monster Finishing Guidelines" on page 10 for detailed finishing directions. Go ahead and attach safety eyes now. Make sure to attach 1 eye through center of eye patch.

You're done! Now, have some fun and go raid the dress-up box with Dot. And put *Breakfast at Tiffany's* in the DVD player. The only thing that will make Dot happier is if you have some champagne and cupcakes ready for the movie, too!

Leila, Lydia, & Lucas
the Momma and Baby Monsters

Leila, Lydia, and Lucas are one big happy monster family. Lydia and Lucas, the monster kids, absolutely love jumping on beds, so that's where the family tends to hang out most of the time. Leila, the momma monster, doesn't mind this since she generally just sits back, snuggles in the pillows on the bed, and lets the kids do their thing. If they get too rowdy or wild, she tells them it's time to calm down and makes them take a nap while riding in her pockets. But, most of the time they manage to bounce their energy out after a few minutes and they end up coming over, cuddling up in the pillows with her, and falling asleep for several hours.

Materials

It's easy to use any yarn-and-needle combination for this project. To find out more, see "What's the Deal with Gauge?" (page 5).

220–280 yards of yarn in main color (MC)

120–180 yards of yarn in contrasting color (CC)

1 set of double-pointed needles 2 or 3 sizes smaller than those recommended for yarn

Circular needle (36" or longer) in same size as dpns

4 removable stitch markers or small pieces of waste yarn

Notions: tapestry needle, plastic safety eyes, white felt for teeth, fabric glue, stuffing, row counter (optional), stitch marker, straight pins (optional)

Samples

Green-and-Aqua Leila, Lydia, and Lucas

Finished sizes: Momma: 15" tall, Babies: 6½" tall

MC 1 skein of Cascade 220 Wool from Cascade Yarns (100% Peruvian Highland wool; 100 g/3.5oz; 220 yds) in color 8903 **[4]**

CC 1 skein of Cascade 220 Wool from Cascade Yarns in color 8908

U.S. size 5 (3.75 mm) needles

Black safety eyes: Momma: 18 mm, Babies: 7 mm

Yellow-and-Orange Leila, Lydia, and Lucas

Finished sizes: Momma: 17" tall, Babies: 8" tall

MC 2 skeins of Comfort from Berroco (50% super fine nylon, 50% super fine acrylic; 100 g/3.5oz; 210 yds/193 m) in color 9712 **[4]**

CC 1 skein of Comfort from Berroco in color 9731

U.S. size 7 (4.5 mm) needles

Black safety eyes: Momma: 18 mm, Babies: 7 mm

Leila (Momma)

BODY

Using the Magic Loop method (page 6), CO 100 sts in MC and join, making sure not to twist sts. PM to indicate beg of rnd.

R1–R10: Knit all sts.

Stop and place removable st marker or tie small piece of different-colored waste yarn to sts 5, 23, 28, and 46 (this marks where you will pick up sts for pockets when you finish body).

R11–R50: Knit all sts.

R51: (K2tog, K48) twice. (98 sts)

R52: Knit all sts.

R53: (K47, K2tog) twice. (96 sts)

R54: Knit all sts.

R55: (K2tog, K46) twice. (94 sts)

R56: Knit all sts.

R57: (K45, K2tog) twice. (92 sts)

R58: Knit all sts.

R59: (K2tog, K44) twice. (90 sts)

R60: Knit all sts.

R61: (K43, K2tog) twice. (88 sts)

R62: Knit all sts.

R63: (K2tog, K42) twice. (86 sts)

R64: Knit all sts.

R65: (K41, K2tog) twice. (84 sts)

R66: Knit all sts.

R67: (K2tog, K38, K2tog) twice. (80 sts)

R68: (K2tog, K36, K2tog) twice. (76 sts)

R69: (K2tog, K34, K2tog) twice. (72 sts)

R70: (K2tog, K32, K2tog) twice. (68 sts)

R71: (K2tog, K30, K2tog) twice. (64 sts)

Turn Leila inside out and work 3-needle BO on all sts. Turn Leila RS out and get ready for more serious monster knitting!

POCKET (MAKE 2.)

Using st markers you added on R10 of body as guide and using CC, PU 18 sts between first and second st markers (fig. 1).

R1–R20: Beg with knit row, work back and forth in St st.

R21–R24: (K1, P1) across.

R25: BO all sts in patt.

Sew sides of pocket to body with a running stitch.

Now, PU 18 sts between third and fourth st markers and rep above instructions to make second pocket.

LEG (MAKE 2.)

Using dpns, evenly CO 14 sts in CC and join, making sure not to twist sts. PM to indicate beg of rnd.

R1–R35: Knit all sts.

Place first 7 sts of rnd on 1 needle and second 7 sts on second needle.

Work heel with last 7 sts.

R1: Sl1p, purl to end, turn.

R2: Sl1k, knit to end, turn.

R3: Sl1p, purl to end, turn.

R4: Sl1k, knit to end, turn.

R5: Sl1p, purl to end, turn.

Beg foot

R1: PM, this will become new beg of rnd. Knit across heel sts once more. Using new dpn, PU 3 sts from left side of heel flap, knit across half of held instep sts with same needle, knit across rest of held instep sts on third dpn, and PU 3 sts from right side of heel flap with same needle (fig. 2). (20 sts)

R2: Knit all sts.

R3: (K6, K2tog, K2tog) twice. (16 sts)

R4: Knit all sts.

R5: (K6, K2tog) twice. (14 sts)

R6: Knit all sts.

R7: (K6, K1f&b) twice. (16 sts)

R8: Knit all sts.

R9: (K7, K1f&b) twice. (18 sts)

Picking up stitches for pocket

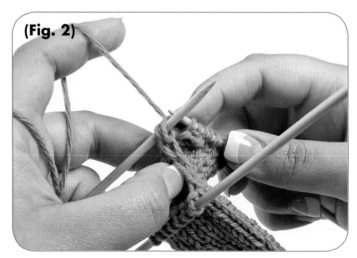

Picking up stitches on heel flap

R10: Knit all sts.

R11: (K8, K1f&b) twice. (20 sts)

R12–R19: Knit all sts.

R20: (K6, K2tog, K2tog) twice. (16 sts)

Cut yarn and with tapestry needle, use Kitchener st to close foot.

ARM (MAKE 2.)

Using dpns, evenly CO 14 sts in MC and join, making sure not to twist sts. PM to indicate beg of rnd.

R1–R30: Knit all sts.

R31: K2tog around. (7 sts)

Cut yarn and using tapestry needle, thread through rem sts to close hand.

Lydia and Lucas (Babies)

BODY (MAKE 2.)

Using the Magic Loop method (page 6), CO 30 sts in CC and join, making sure not to twist sts. PM to indicate beg of rnd.

R1–R20: Knit all sts.

R21: (K2tog, K11, K2tog) twice. (26 sts)

R22: (K2tog, K9, K2tog) twice. (22 sts)

R23: (K2tog, K7, K2tog) twice. (18 sts)

Turn body inside out and work 3-needle BO on all sts. Turn RS out and keep knitting!

ARM (MAKE 4.)

Using dpns, evenly CO 9 sts in CC and join, making sure not to twist sts. PM to indicate beg of rnd.

R1–R12: Knit all sts.

Cut yarn and using tapestry needle, thread through rem sts to close hand.

LEG (MAKE 4.)

Using dpns, evenly CO 6 sts in MC and join, making sure not to twist sts. PM to indicate beg of rnd. (If you prefer you can most likely successfully knit these 6 sts as an I-cord on 1 needle.)

R1–R15: Knit all sts.

Place first 2 sts of rnd on 1 needle and next 4 sts on second needle.

Work the heel with the last 4 sts.

R1: Sl1p, purl to end, turn.

R2: Sl1k, knit to end, turn.

R3: Sl1p, purl to end, turn.

R4: Sl1k, knit to end, turn.

R5: Sl1p, purl to end, turn.

Beg foot

R1: PM, this will be become your new beg of rnd. Knit across the heel sts once more. Using a new dpn, PU 2 sts from left side of heel flap, knit across half of held instep sts with same needle, knit across rest of held instep sts on a third dpn and PU 2 sts from right side of heel flap with same needle. (10 sts)

R2: (K3, K2tog) twice. (8 sts)

R3–R8: Knit all sts.

Stuff foot, cut yarn, and using a tapestry needle, thread through rem sts to close foot.

Finishing

Are you ready to bring your monster to life? Turn to "General Monster Finishing Guidelines" on page 10 for detailed finishing directions.

Way to go! That was a big project, knitting a whole monster family! Why don't you go hop on the bed with Lydia and Lucas to celebrate? Or, maybe sitting in the pillows with Leila is more your style. Either way, it's going to be hard not to smile when you see a whole monster family hanging out on your bed!

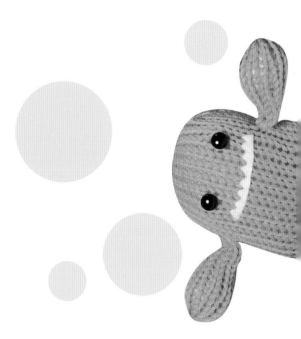

Petunia
the Patio Monster

Petunia's favorite place is sitting on the patio on a gloriously sunny day, soaking up rays. She lives for the summer and is particularly fond of eating finger sandwiches and drinking lemonade to celebrate while the sun beams down from the sky. Petunia has done everything in her power to eliminate stress and make her life as simple as possible so she can spend hours outside just sitting to take advantage of the sun. She also practices her own form of a sun dance by making a new pitcher of lemonade every morning, just so she's prepared in case the sun comes out!

Materials

It's easy to use any yarn-and-needle combination for this project. To find out more, see "What's the Deal with Gauge?" (page 5).

130–180 yards of yarn

1 set of double-pointed needles 2 or 3 sizes smaller than those recommended for yarn

Circular needle (36" or longer) in same size as dpns

Notions: tapestry needle, plastic safety eyes, white felt for teeth, fabric glue, stuffing, row counter (optional), stitch marker, straight pins (optional)

Samples

Pink Petunia
Finished size: 23" tall

2 skeins of Sprout from the Verde Collection by Classic Elite Yarns (100% organic cotton; 100 g; 109 yds) in color 4389 (**5**)

U.S. size 9 (5.5 mm) needles

15 mm black safety eyes

Green Petunia
Finished size: 16" tall

1 skein of 220 Superwash from Cascade Yarns (100% superwash wool; 100 g/3.5 oz; 220 yds) in color 886 (**3**)

U.S. size 5 (3.75 mm) needles

12 mm black safety eyes

Body

Using the Magic Loop method (page 6), CO 48 sts and join, making sure not to twist sts. PM to indicate beg of rnd.

R1–R50: Knit all sts.

R51: (K2tog, K22) twice. (46 sts)

R52: Knit all sts.

R53: (K21, K2tog) twice. (44 sts)

R54: Knit all sts.

R55: (K2tog, K20) twice. (42 sts)

R56: Knit all sts.

R57: (K19, K2tog) twice. (40 sts)

R58: Knit all sts.

R59: (K2tog, K18) twice. (38 sts)

R60: Knit all sts.

R61: (K17, K2tog) twice. (36 sts)

R62: (K2tog, K14, K2tog) twice. (32 sts)

R63: (K2tog, K12, K2tog) twice. (28 sts)

R64: (K2tog, K10, K2tog) twice. (24 sts)

R65: (K2tog, K8, K2tog) twice. (20 sts)

Turn Petunia inside out and work 3-needle BO on all sts. Turn Petunia RS out and there you go—a monster body!

Arm (Make 2.)

Using dpns, evenly CO 6 sts and join, making sure not to twist sts. PM to indicate beg of rnd.

R1: K1f&b all sts. (12 sts)

R2: (K1f&b, K1) around. (18 sts)

R3–R14: Knit all sts.

R15: (K2tog, K7) twice. (16 sts)

R16–R19: Knit all sts.

R20: (K6, K2tog) twice. (14 sts)

R21–R24: Knit all sts.

R25: (K2tog, K5) twice. (12 sts)

R26–R29: Knit all sts.

R30: (K4, K2tog) twice. (10 sts)

R31–R35: Knit all sts.

R36: BO all sts.

Leg (Make 2.)

Using dpns, evenly CO 6 sts and join, making sure not to twist sts. PM to indicate beg of rnd.

R1: K1f&b all sts. (12 sts)

R2: (K1f&b, K1) around. (18 sts)

R3–R17: Knit all sts.

R18: (K2tog, K7) twice. (16 sts)

R19–R27: Knit all sts.

R28: (K6, K2tog) twice. (14 sts)

R29–R37: Knit all sts.

R38: (K2tog, K5) twice. (12 sts)

R39–R47: Knit all sts.

R48: (K4, K2tog) twice. (10 sts)

R49–R52: Knit all sts.

R53: BO all sts.

Finishing

Are you ready to bring your monster to life? Turn to "General Monster Finishing Guidelines" on page 10 for detailed finishing directions.

Great job, you awesome monster knitter, you! You might want to use this as an opportunity to go sit out in the sun with Petunia and take a break from your knitting. If there's no sun at your house right now, you could make some lemonade and finger sandwiches to share with Petunia and turn on all the lights and pretend there's sun!

Gabby the Garden Monster

Gabby currently resides in a lovely vegetable garden. She's a socially awkward monster and feels most comfortable talking to fruits and vegetables. In particular she likes tomatoes (I think she sees some family resemblance there, but she denies it every time I ask), but she's more than happy to talk to lettuce, zucchini, broccoli, snap peas, and even carrots. She enjoys cracking jokes with the veggies. Her favorite joke, the one that keeps her rolling on the ground with laughter for hours? "What did the garden vegetables say? Lettuce, turnip, and pea!"

Materials

It's easy to use any yarn-and-needle combination for this project. To find out more, see "What's the Deal with Gauge?" (page 5).

100–140 yards of yarn

1 set of double-pointed needles 2 or 3 sizes smaller than those recommended for yarn

Notions: tapestry needle, plastic safety eyes, white felt for teeth, fabric glue, stuffing, row counter (optional), stitch marker, straight pins (optional)

Samples

Red Gabby

Finished size: 8" tall

2 skeins of Sprout from the Verde Collection by Classic Elite Yarns (100% organic cotton; 100 g; 109 yds) in color 4358 [5]

U.S. size 9 (5.5 mm) needles

12 mm black safety eyes

Pink Gabby

Finished size: 6" tall

1 skein of 220 Wool from Cascade Yarns (100% Peruvian Highland wool; 100 g/3.5 oz; 220 yds) in color 9477 [4]

U.S. size 5 (3.75 mm) needles

9 mm black safety eyes

Body

Using dpns, evenly CO 6 sts and join, making sure not to twist sts. PM to indicate beg of rnd.

R1: K1f&b all sts. (12 sts)

R2: K1f&b all sts. (24 sts)

R3: Knit all sts.

R4: (K1f&b, K1) around. (36 sts)

R5: Knit all sts.

R6: (K1f&b, K2) around. (48 sts)

R7: Knit all sts.

R8: (K1f&b, K3) around. (60 sts)

R9–R28: Knit all sts.

R29: (K1, K2tog) around. (40 sts)

R30: Knit all sts.

R31: K2tog around. (20 sts)

Stop and stuff body. Make sure to add belly button now as well!

R32: K2tog around. (10 sts)

R33 and R34: Knit all sts.

R35: K1f&b around. (20 sts)

R36: Knit all sts.

R37: (K1, K1f&b) around. (30 sts)

R38–R50: Knit all sts.

R51: K2tog around. (15 sts)

Stop again and stuff head and neck. Make sure to attach safety eyes now as well, lining them up so they're centered over belly button.

R52: Knit all sts.

R53: K2tog, ending with K1. (8 sts)

Cut yarn and using tapestry needle, thread through rem sts to close head. I know it just looks like a peanut or mutant tomato now, but if you keep knitting I promise it'll become a monster. Unless you're into mutant tomatoes, in which case by all means, stop now.

Arm (Make 2.)

Using dpns, evenly CO 10 sts and join, making sure not to twist sts. PM to indicate beg of rnd.

R1–R18: Knit all sts.

R19: K1f&b of first 5 sts of rnd, knit to end. (15 sts)

R20–R27: Knit all sts.

R28: K2tog around, end with K1. (8 sts)

Cut yarn and using tapestry needle, thread through rem sts to close hand.

Ear (Make 2.)

Using dpns, evenly CO 8 sts and join, making sure not to twist sts. PM to indicate beg of rnd.

R1: Knit all sts.

R2: (K1f&b, K3) twice. (10 sts)

R3: Knit all sts.

R4: (K4, K1f&b) twice. (12 sts)

R5–R15: Knit all sts.

R16: K2tog around. (6 sts)

Cut yarn and using tapestry needle, thread through rem sts to close ear.

Foot (Make 2.)

Using dpns, evenly CO 10 sts and join, making sure not to twist sts. PM to indicate beg of rnd.

R1: Knit all sts.

R2: (K1f&b, K4) twice. (12 sts)

R3: Knit all sts.

R4: (K5, K1f&b) twice. (14 sts)

R5: Knit all sts.

R6: (K1f&b, K6) twice. (16 sts)

R7: Knit all sts.

R8: (K7, K1f&b) twice. (18 sts)

R9–R15: Knit all sts.

R16: K2tog around. (9 sts)

Cut yarn and using tapestry needle, thread through rem sts to close foot.

Finishing

Are you ready to bring your monster to life? Turn to "General Monster Finishing Guidelines" on page 10 for detailed finishing directions.

There you go, a vegetable-garden monster. If you don't have a vegetable garden, do be warned that Gabby will try to live in your refrigerator to talk to the fruits and veggies you have in there instead. If this is the case, you might want to knit her a nice little hat and scarf to keep her cozy and warm.

Hugo
the Couch Potato Monster

Hugo is a big monster with an even bigger heart. No matter what time of day it is, you can pretty much always find Hugo snoozing on the couch, hoping someone will come sit down next to him so he can cuddle. All Hugo really wants out of life is to snuggle up on the couch, watch movies, and eat popcorn all day. He also really likes hugs, and will hug everyone he can as often as possible.

Materials

It's easy to use any yarn-and-needle combination for this project. To find out more, see "What's the Deal with Gauge?" (page 5).

250–300 yards of yarn

1 set of double-pointed needles 2 or 3 sizes smaller than those recommended for yarn

Circular needle (36" or longer) in same size as dpns

Notions: tapestry needle, plastic safety eyes, white felt for teeth, fabric glue, stuffing, row counter (optional), stitch marker, straight pins (optional)

Samples

Orange Hugo

Finished size: 18" tall

2 skeins of Comfort Chunky from Berroco (50% super fine nylon, 50% super fine acrylic; 100 g/3.5 oz; 150 yds/138 m) in color 574 (5)

U.S. size 9 (5.5 mm) needles

18 mm black safety eyes

Bright Aqua Hugo

Finished size: 14" tall

1 skein of Cascade 220 Wool from Cascade Yarns (100% Peruvian Highland wool; 100 g/3.5 oz; 220 yds) in color 7812 (4)

U.S. size 5 (3.75 mm) needles

15 mm black safety eyes

Leg (Make 2.)

Using dpns, evenly CO 6 sts and join, making sure not to twist sts. PM to indicate beg of rnd.

R1: K1f&b all sts. (12 sts)

R2: K1f&b all sts. (24 sts)

R3: (K1f&b, K3) around. (30 sts)

R4–R24: Knit all sts.

At end of rnd 24, backward-loop CO 15 sts and cut yarn. (45 sts)

Following instructions in "The Legs to Body Situation" (page 8), transfer leg sts to circular needle as follows. For first leg, put 15 sts on front needle and 30 sts (15 leg plus 15 CO) on back needle. For second leg, again make sure to cut yarn, and put 30 sts (15 leg plus 15 CO) on front needle and 15 sts on back needle. You'll have 90 total sts and new beg of rnd in middle of Hugo's second leg.

Body

Using Magic Loop method (page 6), PM to indicate beg of rnd, and beg.

R1–R60: Knit all sts.

R61: (K2tog, K43) twice. (88 sts)

R62: Knit all sts.

R63: (K42, K2tog) twice. (86 sts)

R64: Knit all sts.

R65: (K2tog, K41) twice. (84 sts)

R66: Knit all sts.

R67: (K40, K2tog) twice. (82 sts)

R68: Knit all sts.

R69: (K2tog, K39) twice. (80 sts)

R70: Knit all sts.

R71: (K38, K2tog) twice. (78 sts)

R72: Knit all sts.

R73: (K2tog, K37) twice. (76 sts)

R74: Knit all sts.

R75: (K36, K2tog) twice. (74 sts)

R76: Knit all sts.

R77: (K2tog, K35) twice. (72 sts)

R78: Knit all sts.

R79: (K34, K2tog) twice. (70 sts)

R80: Knit all sts.

R81: (K2tog, K33) twice. (68 sts)

R82: Knit all sts.

R83: (K32, K2tog) twice. (66 sts)

R84: Knit all sts.

R85: (K2tog, K29, K2tog) twice. (62 sts)

R86: (K2tog, K27, K2tog) twice. (58 sts)

R87: (K2tog, K25, K2tog) twice. (54 sts)

R88: (K2tog, K23, K2tog) twice. (50 sts)

Turn Hugo inside out and work 3-needle BO on all sts. Turn Hugo RS out and give yourself a round of applause for getting through that many monster sts!

Arm (Make 2.)

Using dpns, evenly CO 6 sts, PM, and join, making sure not to twist sts.

R1: K1f&b all sts. (12 sts)

R2: K1f&b all sts. (24 sts)

R3–R30: Knit all sts.

R31: BO all sts.

Finishing

Are you ready to bring your monster to life? Turn to "General Monster Finishing Guidelines" on page 10 for detailed finishing directions.

That's it! You've made a big, cuddly monster! Make sure that Hugo has his own spot on your couch with lots of pillows and blankets and you'll make Hugo a happy guy. You could also throw in a movie, pop up some popcorn, snuggle up next to Hugo, and knit him some friends if you want to make him really, really happy.

Coco
the Canister Monster

Coco is a little monster. She lives in my kitchen canisters, hopping from sugar, to flour, to tea. My guess is that she's constantly waiting for me to make chocolate chip cookies so she can sneak into the canister where they're stored and eat them all before anyone else gets any. I know it seems surprising that such a tiny monster would be able to eat an entire batch of cookies by herself, but I tell you she can do it. I believe it's something like a snake being able to dislocate its jaw so it can fit bigger food in its mouth. I think she can do that with her stomach somehow.

Materials

It's easy to use any yarn-and-needle combination for this project. To find out more, see "What's the Deal with Gauge?" (page 5).

50–90 yards of yarn

1 set of double-pointed needles 2 or 3 sizes smaller than those recommended for yarn

Circular needle (36" or longer) in same size as dpns

Notions: tapestry needle, plastic safety eyes, white felt for teeth, fabric glue, stuffing, row counter (optional), stitch marker, straight pins (optional)

Samples

Green Coco

Finished size: 7" tall

1 skein of Ariosa from Classic Elite Yarns (90% extra fine merino, 10% cashmere; 50 g; 87 yds) in color 9465B **5**

U.S. size 9 (5.5 mm) needles

9 mm black safety eyes

Orange Coco

Finished size: 12" tall

1 skein of Magnum from Cascade Yarns (100% Peruvian Highland wool; 250 g/8.82 oz; 123 yds) in color 825 **6**

U.S. size 13 (9 mm) needles

15 mm black safety eyes

Blue Coco

Finished size: 6" tall

1 skein of Mulberry Merino from Plymouth Yarn Company (52% mulberry silk, 48% merino wool; 50 g; 99 yds) in color 7020 **4**

U.S. size 5 (3.75 mm) needles

9 mm black safety eyes

Leg (Make 2.)

Using dpns, evenly CO 4 sts and join, making sure not to twist sts. PM to indicate beg of rnd.

R1: K1f&b all sts. (8 sts)

R2: (K1f&b, K1) around. (12 sts)

R3–R12: Knit all sts.

R13: K1f&b, knit to the last st, K1f&b. (14 sts)

R14: Knit all sts.

R15: K1f&b, knit to the last st, K1f&b. (16 sts)

R16: Knit all sts.

At end of rnd 16, backward-loop CO 2 sts and cut yarn. (18 sts)

Following instructions in "The Legs to Body Situation" (page 8), transfer leg sts to circular needle as follows. For first leg, put 8 sts on front needle and 10 sts (8 leg plus 2 CO) on back needle. For second leg, again make sure to cut yarn, and put 10 sts (8 leg plus 2 CO) on front needle and 8 sts on back needle. You'll have 36 total sts and new beg of rnd in middle of Coco's second leg.

Body

Using Magic Loop method (page 6), PM to indicate beg of rnd, and beg.

R1–R15: Knit all sts.

R16: (K2tog, K16) twice. (34 sts)

R17: Knit all sts.

R18: (K15, K2tog) twice. (32 sts)

R19: Knit all sts.

R20: (K2tog, K14) twice. (30 sts)

R21: Knit all sts.

R22: (K13, K2tog) twice. (28 sts)

R23: Knit all sts.

R24: (K2tog, K12) twice. (26 sts)

R25: Knit all sts.

R26: (K11, K2tog) twice. (24 sts)

R27: Knit all sts.

R28: (K2tog, K8, K2tog) twice. (20 sts)

R29: (K2tog, K6, K2tog) twice. (16 sts)

Cut yarn, turn Coco inside out, and work 3-needle BO on all sts. Turn Coco RS out and smile at your tiny little monster!

Arm (Make 2.)

Using dpns, evenly CO 4 sts and join, making sure not to twist sts. PM to indicate beg of rnd.

R1: K1f&b of all sts. (8 sts)

R2: (K1f&b, K1) around. (12 sts)

R3–R8: Knit all sts.

R9: (K2tog, K4) twice. (10 sts)

R10 and R11: Knit all sts.

R12: (K3, K2tog) twice. (8 sts)

R13–R16: Knit all sts.

R17: BO all sts.

Finishing

Are you ready to bring your monster to life? Turn to "General Monster Finishing Guidelines" on page 10 for detailed finishing directions.

Way to go, tiny-monster maker! Why is it that the smaller the monster, the cuter it seems to be? Yeah, well, just like my pug Lucy, Coco uses her size to her advantage, so be warned. Although, I must say that more chocolate chip cookies get made in my house since she moved into my kitchen.

Gort the Gym Bag Monster

Gort is a sports and fitness fanatic. His favorite sport is basketball and he's always wanted to play in the NBA, but unfortunately most teams won't let monsters play. To make up for it he lives in a gym bag so that he can sneak rides to the gym and at least be around other like-minded fitness folks for a few hours here and there (though he hasn't found anyone who goes to the gym as much as he would like). He also likes living in the gym bag since he has a secret obsession for the smell of dirty sweat socks, but that's a different issue altogether!

Materials

It's easy to use any yarn-and-needle combination for this project. To find out more, see "What's the Deal with Gauge?" (page 5).

100–140 yards of yarn in main color (MC)

85–125 yards of yarn in contrasting color (CC)

1 set of double-pointed needles 2 or 3 sizes smaller than those recommended for yarn

Circular needle (36" or longer) in same size as dpns

Notions: tapestry needle, plastic safety eyes, white felt for teeth, fabric glue, stuffing, row counter (optional), stitch marker, straight pins (optional)

Samples

Red-and-Blue Gort

Finished size: 16" tall

MC 1 skein of Comfort from Berroco (50% super fine nylon, 50% super fine acrylic; 100 g/3.5 oz; 210 yds/138 m) in color 9750 [4]

CC 1 skein of Comfort from Berroco in color 9714

U.S. size 7 (4.5 mm) needles

15 mm black safety eyes

Pink-and-Green Gort

Finished size: 13" tall

MC 1 skein of 220 Superwash from Cascade Yarns (100% superwash wool; 100 g/3.5 oz; 220 yds) in color 886 [3]

CC 1 skein of 220 Superwash from Cascade Yarns in color 835

U.S. size 5 (3.75 mm) needles

12 mm black safety eyes

Leg (Make 2.)

Using dpns, evenly CO 5 sts in MC and join, making sure not to twist sts. PM to indicate beg of rnd.

R1: K1f&b all sts in MC. (10 sts)

R2: K1f&b all sts in MC. (20 sts)

R3 and R4: Knit all sts in MC.

R5–R25: Knit all sts in 3 rnds CC, 3 rnds MC, ending in third rnd CC.

R26: Cont in MC: K1f&b, K18, K1f&b of last st. (22 sts)

R27: Knit all sts.

R28: K1f&b of first 2 sts, K18, K1f&b of last 2 sts. (26 sts)

At end of rnd 28, backward-loop CO 4 sts and cut yarn. (30 sts)

Following instructions in "The Legs to Body Situation" (page 8), transfer leg sts to circular needle as follows. For first leg, put 13 sts on front needle and 17 sts (13 leg plus 4 CO) on back needle. For second leg, again make sure to cut yarn, and put 17 sts (13 leg plus 4 CO) on front needle and 13 sts on back needle. You will have 60 total sts and new beg of rnd in middle of Gort's second leg.

Body

Using Magic Loop method (page 6), PM to indicate beg of rnd, and beg.

R1–R54: Beg in CC, knit all sts in 3 rnds CC, 3 rnds MC, cont this patt throughout whole body.

R55: (CC) (K2tog, K28) twice. (58 sts)

R56: Knit all sts.

R57: (K27, K2tog) twice. (56 sts)

R58: Knit all sts.

R59: (K2tog, K26) twice. (54 sts)

R60: Knit all sts.

R61: (K25, K2tog) twice. (52 sts)

R62: Knit all sts.

R63: (K2tog, K24) twice. (50 sts)

R64: Knit all sts.

R65: (K23, K2tog) twice. (48 sts)

R66: Knit all sts.

R67: (K2tog, K22) twice. (46 sts)

R68: Knit all sts.

R69: (K21, K2tog) twice. (44 sts)

R70: Knit all sts.

R71: (K2tog, K20) twice. (42 sts)

R72: Knit all sts.

R73: (K19, K2tog) twice. (40 sts)

R74: Knit all sts.

R75: (K2tog, K16, K2tog) twice. (36 sts)

R76: (K2tog, K14, K2tog) twice. (32 sts)

R77: (K2tog, K12, K2tog) twice. (28 sts)

R78: (K2tog, K10, K2tog) twice. (24 sts)

Turn Gort inside out and work 3-needle BO on all sts. Turn Gort RS out and get ready for more striped knitting.

Arm (Make 2.)

Using dpns, evenly CO 12 sts in MC and join, making sure not to twist sts. PM to indicate beg of rnd.

R1–R43: Knit all sts in 3 rnds MC, 3 rnds CC, ending with 2 rnds MC.

R44: With MC, K1f&b of all sts. (24 sts)

R45–R55: Starting with 3 rnds CC, knit all sts and cont in established patt, ending with 2 rnds MC.

R56: With MC, K2tog around. (12 sts)

R57: With MC, K2tog around. (6 sts)

Cut yarn and using tapestry needle, thread through rem sts to close hand.

Finishing

Are you ready to bring your monster to life? Turn to "General Monster Finishing Guidelines" on page 10 for detailed finishing directions.

Huzzah! A finished sporty monster. Make sure Gort gets lots of time to exercise, since he gets very cranky if he's not being sporty. You might actually want to make him some fitness-minded monster buddies so he has other monsters to play with. You could even make a whole basketball team's worth of friends so he can be in the MBA (Monster Basketball Association). Just watch him with your socks; he can get a little weird about them.

Toothy Joe
the Mailbox Monster

Toothy Joe is a very funny monster that I found living in my mailbox when I moved to my new house. He really likes the mailbox because every day all sorts of interesting stuff comes for him to play with. He loves to look through the weekly flyers and he tries to figure out what's in each envelope by holding it up to his forehead like Johnny Carson. He also *loves* magazines. And, when he's feeling particularly sassy, he'll use his one tooth to bite and chew on the mail, since that always gets a reaction that makes him laugh for hours and hours. Living in the mailbox has other perks too: Toothy Joe jumps out and scares the mailman every day!

Materials

It's easy to use any yarn-and-needle combination for this project. To find out more, see "What's the Deal with Gauge?" (page 5).

130–180 yards of yarn in main color (MC)
60–110 yards of yarn in contrasting color (CC)
1 set of double-pointed needles 2 or 3 sizes smaller than those recommended for yarn
Circular needle (36" or longer) in same size as dpns
Notions: tapestry needle, plastic safety eyes, white felt for teeth, fabric glue, stuffing, row counter (optional), stitch marker, straight pins (optional)

Samples

Orange-and-Aqua Toothy Joe

Finished size: 16" tall

MC 1 skein of Sweater from Spud and Chloë (55% superwash wool, 45% organic cotton; 100 g; 160 yds /146 m) in color 7508 **4**

CC 1 skein of Sweater from Spud and Chloe in color 7510

U.S. size 7 (4.5 mm) needles
15 mm black safety eyes

Green-and-Purple Toothy Joe

Finished size: 20" tall

MC 2 skeins of Cascade 220 Wool from Cascade Yarns (100% Peruvian Highland wool; 100 g/3.5 oz; 220 yds) in color 8914 **4**

CC 1 skein of Cascade 220 Wool from Cascade Yarns in color 8909

U.S. size 9 (5.5 mm) needles (2 strands held tog)
18 mm black safety eyes

Body

Using circular needle, CO 24 sts in CC. Do not join.

R1–R17: Beg with purl row, work back and forth in St st.

R18: Switch to MC, CO 6 sts, knit across established sts, and backward-loop CO an additional 42 sts. (72 sts)

R19–R44: Using the Magic Loop method (page 6), join, making sure not to twist sts. PM to indicate beg of rnd, and knit all sts.

R45: Knit first 36 sts of rnd, BO last 36 sts.

R46: K36, PU 36 sts along BO edge through both loops. The last 2 rnds create a line that will become Toothy Joe's mouth.

R47: Knit all sts.

R48: (K2tog, K34) twice. (70 sts)

R49: Knit all sts.

R50: (K33, K2tog) twice. (68 sts)

R51: Knit all sts.

R52: (K2tog, K32) twice. (66 sts)

R53: Knit all sts.

R54: (K31, K2tog) twice. (64 sts)

R55: Knit all sts.

R56: (K2tog, K30) twice. (62 sts)

R57: Knit all sts.

R58: (K29, K2tog) twice. (60 sts)

R59: Knit all sts.

R60: (K2tog, K28) twice. (58 sts)

R61: Knit all sts.

R62: (K27, K2tog) twice. (56 sts)

R63: Knit all sts.

R64: (K2tog, K24, K2tog) twice. (52 sts)

R65: Knit all sts.

R66: (K2tog, K22, K2tog) twice. (48 sts)

Turn Toothy Joe inside out and work 3-needle BO on all sts. Turn Joe RS out and give yourself a round of applause for your magnificent monster knitting!

Arm (Make 2.)

Using dpns, evenly CO 10 sts in MC and join, making sure not to twist sts. PM to indicate beg of rnd.

R1–R28: Knit all sts.

R29: K1f&b all sts. (20 sts)

R30–R38: Knit all sts.

R39: K2tog around. (10 sts)

R40: K2tog around. (5 sts)

Cut yarn and using tapestry needle, thread through rem sts to close hand.

Leg (Make 2.)

Using dpns, evenly CO 12 sts in CC and join, making sure not to twist sts. PM to indicate beg of rnd.

R1–R3: Knit all sts in CC.

R4–R51: Knit all sts in 2 rnds MC, 2 rnds CC (you'll be ending with CC rnd; cont in CC to end).

Place first 6 sts of rnd on 1 needle and second 6 sts on second needle.

Work heel with last 6 sts.

R1: Sl1p, purl to end, turn.

R2: Sl1k, knit to end, turn.

R3: Sl1p, purl to end, turn.

R4: Sl1k, knit to end, turn.

R5: Sl1p, purl to end, turn.

Beg foot

R1: PM, this will become new beg of rnd. Knit across heel sts once more. Using new dpn, PU 3 sts from left side of heel flap, knit across half of held instep sts with same needle, knit across rest of held instep sts on third dpn, and PU 3 sts from right side of heel flap with same needle (fig. 1). (18 sts)

R2: Knit all sts.

R3: (K5, K2tog, K2tog) twice. (14 sts)

R4: Knit all sts.

R5: (K5, K2tog) twice. (12 sts)

R6 and R7: Knit all sts.

R8: K4, K1f&b, K6, K1f&b. (14 sts)

R9–R15: Knit all sts.

Cut yarn and with tapestry needle, use Kitchener st to close foot.

Finishing

Are you ready to bring your monster to life? Turn to "General Monster Finishing Guidelines" on page 10 for detailed finishing directions.

Sew up 2 sides of base before attempting to attach legs so you know where center of base/body is going to be first. Then, sew legs to flap edge to connect them and sew flap shut to finish up body (fig. 2).

You rock, monster knitter! Now, hand Toothy Joe some junk mail and set him on the couch. See if you can't keep him out of your mailbox since most mail carriers don't appreciate it when a monster jumps out when they're attempting to deliver mail, and they might retaliate by stopping your mail.

(Fig. 1)

Picking up stitches on heel flap

(Fig. 2)

Toothy Joe's base flap

Bea the Basement Monster

Bea is an excruciatingly shy monster. Though she absolutely loves humans, she's totally terrified of meeting new people. She lives in the basement so that she can meet new people and be around the ones she knows on her own terms. She really enjoys being alone and generally spends many hours a day organizing everything around her while quietly singing Beatles songs to herself.

Materials

It's easy to use any yarn-and-needle combination for this project. To find out more, see "What's the Deal with Gauge?" (page 5).

200–250 yards of yarn in main color (MC)

80–110 yards of yarn in contrasting color (CC)

1 set of double-pointed needles 2 or 3 sizes smaller than those recommended for yarn

Circular needle (36" or longer) in same size as dpns

Notions: tapestry needle, plastic safety eyes, white felt for teeth, fabric glue, stuffing, row counter (optional), stitch marker, straight pins (optional)

Samples

Orange-and-Green Bea

Finished size: 14" tall

MC 2 skeins of Montera from Classic Elite Yarns (50% llama, 50% wool; 100 g; 127 yds) in color 3833 (4)

CC 1 skein of Montera from Classic Elite Yarns in color 3823

U.S. size 7 (4.5 mm) needles

18 mm black safety eyes

Pink-and-Magenta Bea

Finished size: 12" tall

MC 1 skein of Cascade 220 Wool from Cascade Yarns (100% Peruvian Highland wool; 100 g/3.5 oz; 220 yds) in color 9477 (4)

CC 1 skein of Cascade 220 Wool from Cascade Yarns in color 7801

U.S. size 9 (5.5 mm) needles (2 strands held tog)

18 mm black safety eyes

Body

Using circular needle, CO 30 sts in CC. Do not join.

R1–R23: Beg with purl row, work back and forth in St st.

R24: Switch to MC, CO 8 sts, knit across established sts and backward-loop CO an additional 54 sts. (92 sts)

R25–R75: Using Magic Loop method (page 6), join, making sure not to twist sts. PM to indicate beg of rnd, and knit all sts.

R76: (K2tog, K44) twice. (90 sts)

R77: Knit all sts.

R78: (K43, K2tog) twice. (88 sts)

R79: Knit all sts.

R80: (K2tog, K42) twice. (86 sts)

R81: Knit all sts.

R82: (K41, K2tog) twice. (84 sts)

R83: Knit all sts.

R84: (K2tog, K40) twice. (82 sts)

R85: Knit all sts.

R86: (K39, K2tog) twice. (80 sts)

R87: Knit all sts.

R88: (K2tog, K38) twice. (78 sts)

R89: Knit all sts.

R90: (K37, K2tog) twice. (76 sts)

R91: Knit all sts.

R92: (K2tog, K36) twice. (74 sts)

R93: Knit all sts.

R94: (K35, K2tog) twice. (72 sts)

R95: Knit all sts.

R96: (K2tog, K34) twice. (70 sts)

R97: Knit all sts.

R98: (K33, K2tog) twice. (68 sts)

R99: Knit all sts.

R100: (K2tog, K32) twice. (66 sts)

R101: Knit all sts.

R102: (K31, K2tog) twice. (64 sts)

R103: (K2tog, K28, K2tog) twice. (60 sts)

R104: (K2tog, K26, K2tog) twice. (56 sts)

R105: (K2tog, K24, K2tog) twice. (52 sts)

R106: (K2tog, K22, K2tog) twice. (48 sts)

R107: (K2tog, K20, K2tog) twice. (44 sts)

Turn Bea inside out and work 3-needle BO on all sts. Turn Bea RS out and do a yeah-the-monster-body-is-finished dance!

Arm (Make 2.)

Using dpns, evenly CO 24 sts in MC and join, making sure not to twist sts. PM to indicate beg of rnd.

R1–R30: Knit all sts.

R31: K2tog around. (12 sts)

R32: K2tog around. (6 sts)

Cut yarn and using tapestry needle, thread through rem sts to close arm.

Foot (Make 2.)

Using dpns, evenly CO 18 sts in CC and join, making sure not to twist sts.

PM to indicate beg of rnd.

R1: Knit all sts.

R2: (K1f&b, K8) twice. (20 sts)

R3: Knit all sts.

R4: (K9, K1f&b) twice. (22 sts)

R5: Knit all sts.

R6: (K1f&b, K10) twice. (24 sts)

R7: Knit all sts.

R8: (K11, K1f&b) twice. (26 sts)

R9: Knit all sts.

R10: (K1f&b, K12) twice. (28 sts)

R11: Knit all sts.

R12: (K13, K1f&b) twice. (30 sts)

R13–R22: Knit all sts.

R23: (K2tog, K11, K2tog) twice. (26 sts)

R24: (K2tog, K9, K2tog) twice. (22 sts)

R25: (K2tog, K7, K2tog) twice. (18 sts)

Turn foot inside out and work 3-needle BO on all sts to close.

Ear (Make 2.)

Using dpns, evenly CO 12 sts in CC and join, making sure not to twist sts. PM to indicate beg of rnd.

R1–R5: Knit all sts.

R6: (K1f&b, K5) twice. (14 sts)

R7: Knit all sts.

R8: (K6, K1f&b) twice. (16 sts)

R9: Knit all sts.

R10: (K1f&b, K7) twice. (18 sts)

R11: Knit all sts.

R12: (K8, K1f&b) twice. (20 sts)

R13: Knit all sts.

R14: (K1f&b, K9) twice. (22 sts)

R15: Knit all sts.

R16: (K10, K1f&b) twice. (24 sts)

R17: Knit all sts.

R18: (K1f&b, K11) twice. (26 sts)

R19: Knit all sts.

R20: (K12, K1f&b) twice. (28 sts)

R21–R25: Knit all sts.

Evenly divide sts onto 2 needles and 3-needle BO all sts to close.

Finishing

Are you ready to bring your monster to life? Turn to "General Monster Finishing Guidelines" on page 10 for detailed finishing directions.

Sew up 2 sides of the base before attempting to attach legs so you know where center of base/body is going to be first. Then, sew legs to flap edge to connect them, and sew flap shut to finish up body. See fig. 2 on page 59.

Woot, woot! You're now looking at a finished monster. Don't be too offended if Bea is not as friendly as you would like; just remember that she's very shy. It's best to let her do her own thing—she'll warm up to you and your family over time. And, whether or not she ever admits it to you, she'll always hold a special place in her heart for you since you made her!

Tony has claimed what he thinks is the best home in the entire house: the toy chest! Since he's ball-like in appearance, everyone overlooks him when they look in the toy box, which leaves him undisturbed and able to play all day and all night with any toy he wants. Though Tony doesn't really like to share his toys, he does occasionally enjoy inviting all the other monsters in the house into the toy chest to have big monster parties. He doesn't mind sharing with his friends from time to time, but he doesn't have parties very often so that he can play by himself most of the time and avoid that whole sharing thing.

Materials

It's easy to use any yarn-and-needle combination for this project. To find out more, see "What's the Deal with Gauge?" (page 5).

140–190 yards of yarn

1 set of double-pointed needles 2 or 3 sizes smaller than those recommended for yarn

Notions: tapestry needle, plastic safety eyes, white felt for teeth, fabric glue, stuffing, row counter (optional), stitch marker, straight pins (optional)

Samples

Aqua Tony

Finished size: 13" tall

2 skeins of Comfort Chunky from Berroco (50% super fine nylon, 50% super fine acrylic; 100 g/3.5 oz; 150 yds/138 m) in color 5725 ⑤

U.S. size 9 (5.5 mm) needles

15 mm black safety eyes

Green-and-Blue Tony

Finished size: 10" tall

1 skein of Shepherd Worsted from Lorna's Laces (100% superwash wool; 225 yds) in color 308 Huron ④

U.S. size 6 (4.0 mm) needles

12 mm black safety eyes

Body

Using dpns, evenly CO 6 sts and join, making sure not to twist sts. PM to indicate beg of rnd.

R1: K1f&b all sts. (12 sts)

R2: K1f&b all sts. (24 sts)

R3: (K1, K1f&b) around. (36 sts)

R4: (K2, K1f&b) around. (48 sts)

R5: (K3, K1f&b) around. (60 sts)

R6: (K4, K1f&b) around. (72 sts)

R7–R40: Knit all sts.

R41: (K4, K2tog) around. (60 sts)

R42: (K3, K2tog) around. (48 sts)

R43: (K2, K2tog) around. (36 sts)

R44: (K1, K2tog) around. (24 sts)

Stop and stuff body. Make sure to add belly button and attach safety eyes now as well!

R45: K2tog around. (12 sts)

R46: K2tog around. (6 sts)

Cut yarn and using tapestry needle, thread through rem sts to close head. Tah-dah! You've made a ball with eyes and a belly button.

Arm (Make 2.)

Using dpns, evenly CO 12 sts and join, making sure not to twist sts. PM to indicate beg of rnd.

R1–R20: Knit all sts.

R21: K1f&b of all sts. (24 sts)

R22–R30: Knit all sts.

R31: K2tog around. (12 sts)

R32: K2tog around. (6 sts)

Cut yarn and using tapestry needle, thread through rem sts to close hand.

Leg (Make 2.)

Using dpns, evenly CO 14 sts and join, making sure not to twist sts. PM to indicate beg of rnd.

R1–R35: Knit all sts.

Place first 7 sts of rnd on 1 needle and second 7 sts on second needle.

Work heel with last 7 sts.

R1: Sl1p, purl to end, turn.

R2: Sl1k, knit to end, turn.

R3: Sl1p, purl to end, turn.

R4: Sl1k, knit to end, turn.

R5: Sl1p, purl to end, turn.

R6: Sl1k, knit to end, turn.

R7: Sl1p, purl to end, turn.

Beg foot

R1: PM, this will become new beg of rnd. Knit across heel sts once more. Using new dpn, PU 5 sts from left side of heel flap, knit across half of held instep sts with same needle, knit across rest of held instep sts on third dpn, and PU 5 sts from right side of heel flap with same needle (fig. 1). (24 sts)

R2: Knit all sts.

R3: (K8, K2tog, K2tog) twice. (20 sts)

R4: Knit all sts.

R5: (K8, K2tog) twice. (18 sts)

R6–R16: Knit all sts.

R17: K2tog around. (9 sts)

Cut yarn and using tapestry needle, thread through rem sts to close foot.

Finishing

Are you ready to bring your monster to life? Turn to "General Monster Finishing Guidelines" on page 10 for detailed finishing directions.

There you go, you have made a very roly-poly monster. If you don't have a toy chest, you can just show Tony to the general direction of the toys in your house. He particularly likes Legos and trains, but really he will happily play for hours with anything.

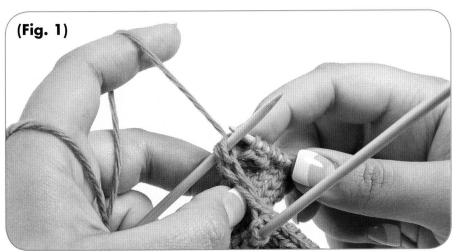

(Fig. 1)

Picking up stitches on heel flap

Kat
the Kitchen Monster

Kat is a monster that lives in my kitchen. She's responsible for moving things in the refrigerator and cabinets, which always seems to create kitchen confusion. Doesn't it always seem like everything in the kitchen moves around and sometimes outright disappears? That's Kat! She likes to stay up at night when everyone else has gone to bed and practice her gourmet cooking skills. She generally gets the kitchen back into shape before the rest of the house gets up, but sometimes she forgets things and leaves them out. She can be blamed for the kitchen always seeming to be a mess—at least in my house!

Materials

It's easy to use any yarn-and-needle combination for this project. To find out more, see "What's the Deal with Gauge?" (page 5).

130–185 yards of yarn

1 set of double-pointed needles 2 or 3 sizes smaller than those recommended for yarn

Circular needle (36" or longer) in same size as dpns

Notions: tapestry needle, plastic safety eyes, white felt for teeth, fabric glue, stuffing, row counter (optional), stitch marker, straight pins (optional), ribbon for Kat's neck (optional)

Samples

Peach Kat
Finished size: 13" tall

1 skein of Dyed Cotton from Blue Sky Alpacas (100% organically grown cotton; 100 g/3.5 oz; 150 yds/138 m) in color 631 **4**

U.S. size 5 (3.75 mm) needles

12 mm black safety eyes

Blue Kat
Finished size: 17" tall

2 skeins of Comfort from Berroco (50% super fine nylon, 50% super fine acrylic; 100 g/3.5 oz; 210 yds/193 m) in color 9714 **4**

U.S. size 9 (5.5 mm) needles (2 strands held tog)

15 mm black safety eyes

Leg

Using dpns, evenly CO 6 sts and join, making sure not to twist sts. PM to indicate beg of rnd.

R1: K1f&b all sts. (12 sts)

R2: (K1f&b, K1) around. (18 sts)

R3–R18: Knit all sts.

R19: K1f&b, K16, and K1f&b of last st. (20 sts)

R20: Knit all sts.

R21: K1f&b, K18, and K1f&b of last st. (22 sts)

R22: Knit all sts.

R23: K1f&b, K20, and K1f&b of last st. (24 sts)

R24: Knit all sts.

At end of rnd 24, backward-loop CO 2 sts and cut yarn. (26 sts)

Following instructions in "The Legs to Body Situation" (page 8), transfer leg sts to circular needle as follows. For first leg, put 12 sts on front needle and 14 sts (12 leg plus 2 CO) on back needle. For second leg, again make sure to cut yarn, and put 14 sts (12 leg plus 2 CO) on front needle and 12 sts on back needle. You will have 52 total sts and new beg of rnd in middle of Kat's second leg.

Body

Using Magic Loop method (page 6), PM to indicate beg of rnd, and beg.

R1–R24: Knit all sts.

R25: (K2tog, K24) twice. (50 sts)

R26: Knit all sts.

R27: (K23, K2tog) twice. (48 sts)

R28: Knit all sts.

R29: (K2tog, K22) twice. (46 sts)

R30: Knit all sts.

R31: (K21, K2tog) twice. (44 sts)

R32: Knit all sts.

R33: (K2tog, K20) twice. (42 sts)

R34: Knit all sts.

R35: (K19, K2tog) twice. (40 sts)

R36: Knit all sts.

R37: (K2tog, K18) twice. (38 sts)

R38: Knit all sts.

R39: (K17, K2tog) twice. (36 sts)

R40: Knit all sts.

R41: (K2tog, K14, K2tog) twice. (32 sts)

R42: (K2tog, K12, K2tog) twice. (28 sts)

R43: (K2tog, K10, K2tog) twice. (24 sts)

R44–R46: Knit all sts.

R47: (K1f&b, K10, K1f&b) twice. (28 sts)

R48: Knit all sts.

R49: (K1f&b, K12, K1f&b) twice. (32 sts)

R50: Knit all sts.

R51: (K1f&b, K14, K1f&b) twice. (36 sts)

R52–R62: Knit all sts.

R63: (K2tog, K14, K2tog) twice. (32 sts)

R64: Knit all sts.

R65: (K2tog, K12, K2tog) twice. (28 sts)

R66: Knit all sts.

R67: (K2tog, K10, K2tog) twice. (24 sts)

R68: Knit all sts.

R69: (K2tog, K8, K2tog) twice. (20 sts)

Turn monster inside out and work 3-needle BO on all sts. Turn Kat RS out and admire your monster handiwork.

Arm (Make 2.)

Using dpns, evenly CO 6 sts and join, making sure not to twist sts. PM to indicate beg of rnd.

R1: K1f&b of all sts. (12 sts)

R2: (K1, K1f&b) around. (18 sts)

R3–R12: Knit all sts.

R13: (K2tog, K7) twice. (16 sts)

R14 and R15: Knit all sts.

R16: (K6, K2tog) twice. (14 sts)

R17 and R18: Knit all sts.

R19: (K2tog, K5) twice. (12 sts)

R20–R34: Knit all sts.

R35: BO all sts.

Ear (Make 2.)

Using dpns, evenly CO 6 sts and join, making sure not to twist sts. PM to indicate beg of rnd.

R1: Knit all sts.

R2: (K1f&b, K2) twice. (8 sts)

R3: Knit all sts.

R4: (K3, K1f&b) twice. (10 sts)

R5: Knit all sts.

R6: (K1f&b, K4) twice. (12 sts)

R7: Knit all sts.

R8: (K5, K1f&b) twice. (14 sts)

R9: Knit all sts.

R10: (K1f&b, K6) twice. (16 sts)

R11: Knit all sts.

R12: (K7, K1f&b) twice. (18 sts)

R13–R16: Knit all sts.

R17: Work 3-needle BO on all sts.

Finishing

Are you ready to bring your monster to life? Turn to "General Monster Finishing Guidelines" on page 10 for detailed finishing directions.

Magnifico, you've got a finished chef monster ready to enroll in cooking school! Now when you find your cookbooks and kitchen supplies in disarray you'll know who's responsible. You might want to encourage Kat's cooking, though; wouldn't it be nice to have a monster as your own personal chef?

Cecil
the Computer Monster

Cecil loves computers. He would spend his entire life surfing the Web if he could, but unfortunately other people in the house need to use the computer and he likes to remain hidden from view. You've probably never seen Cecil himself, but I'm sure you have noticed his mischievous actions. When Cecil is hiding while people are using the computer, he likes to hang out in the computer cables and twist them up. I know we all question how computer cables get so knotted up all the time and we all secretly think that someone must be making things more tangled than they could become on their own. Well, you're right. It's Cecil tangling those cords in hopes that you will spend more time untangling them and give him more time to go online!

Materials

It's easy to use any yarn-and-needle combination for this project. To find out more, see "What's the Deal with Gauge?" (page 5).

140–190 yards of yarn in main color (MC)
100–140 yards of yarn in contrasting color (CC)
1 set of double-pointed needles 2 or 3 sizes smaller than those recommended for yarn
Circular needle (36" or longer) in same size as dpns
Notions: tapestry needle, plastic safety eyes, white felt for teeth, fabric glue, stuffing, row counter (optional), stitch marker, straight pins (optional)

Samples

Pink-and-Green Cecil
Finished size: 18" tall

MC 1 skein of Comfort from Berroco (50% super fine nylon, 50% super fine acrylic; 100 g/3.5 oz; 210 yds/193 m) in color 9710 (**4**)
CC 1 skein of Comfort from Berroco in color 9740
U.S. size 7 (4.5 mm) needles
15 mm black safety eyes

Aqua-and-Red Cecil
Finished size: 17" tall

MC 1 skein of Cascade 220 Wool from Cascade Yarns (100% Peruvian Highland wool; 100 g/3.5 oz; 220 yds) in color 8908 (**4**)
CC 1 skein of Cascade 220 Wool from Cascade Yarns in color 8895
U.S. size 5 (3.75 mm) needles
15 mm black safety eyes

Body

Using the Magic Loop method (page 6), CO 60 sts in MC and join, making sure not to twist sts. PM to indicate beg of rnd.

R1–R9: Knit all sts in MC.

R10–R18: Knit all sts in CC.

R19–R27: Knit all sts in MC.

R28–R36: Knit all sts in CC.

R37–R45: Knit all sts in MC.

R46–R54: Knit all sts in CC.

R55–R57: Knit all sts in MC.

R58: BO first 30 sts of rnd, knit to end of rnd.

R59: PU 30 sts along BO edge through both loops, knit to end of rnd. The last 2 rnds create a line that will become Cecil's mouth. See fig. 1 on page 71.

R60–62: Knit all sts in MC, cont with MC to end of body.

R63: (K2tog, K28) twice. (58 sts)

R64: Knit all sts.

R65: (K27, K2tog) twice. (56 sts)

R66: Knit all sts.

R67: (K2tog, K26) twice. (54 sts)

R68: Knit all sts.

R69: (K25, K2tog) twice. (52 sts)

R70: Knit all sts.

R71: (K2tog, K24) twice. (50 sts)

R72: Knit all sts.

R73: (K23, K2tog) twice. (48 sts)

R74: (K2tog, K20, K2tog) twice. (44 sts)

R75: (K2tog, K18, K2tog) twice. (40 sts)

R76: (K2tog, K16, K2tog) twice. (36 sts)

R77: (K2tog, K14, K2tog) twice. (32 sts)

Turn Cecil inside out and work 3-needle BO on all sts. Turn Cecil RS out and tah-dah! A striped monster body.

Arm (Make 2.)

Using dpns, evenly CO 12 sts in MC and join, making sure not to twist sts. PM to indicate beg of rnd.

R1–R5: Knit all sts in MC.

R6–R10: Knit all sts in CC.

R11–R15: Knit all sts in MC.

R16–R20: Knit all sts in CC.

R21–R25: Knit all sts in MC.

R26–R30: Knit all sts in CC.

R31: Knit all sts in MC, cont in MC to end.

R32: K1f&b all sts. (24 sts)

R33–R42: Knit all sts.

R43: K2tog around. (12 sts)

R44: K2tog around. (6 sts)

Cut yarn and using tapestry needle, thread through rem sts to close hand.

Ear (Make 2.)

The ears are worked entirely in CC.

Using dpns, evenly CO 10 sts and join, making sure not to twist sts. PM to indicate beg of rnd.

R1: Knit all sts.

R2: (K1f&b, K3, K1f&b) twice. (14 sts)

R3: (K1f&b, K5, K1f&b) twice. (18 sts)

R4–R10: Knit all sts.

R11: K2tog around. (9 sts)

Cut yarn and using tapestry needle, thread through rem sts to close ear.

Leg (Make 2.)

Using dpns, evenly CO 16 sts in MC and join, making sure not to twist sts. PM to indicate beg of rnd.

R1–R7: Knit all sts in MC.

R8–R14: Knit all sts in CC.

R15–R21: Knit all sts in MC.

R22–R28: Knit all sts in CC.

R29–R35: Knit all sts in MC.

R36–R42: Knit all sts in CC.

R43 and R44: Knit all sts in MC; cont in MC to end of foot.

Place first 8 sts of rnd on 1 needle and second 8 sts on second needle.

Work heel with last 8 sts.

R1: Sl1p, purl to end, turn.

R2: Sl1k, knit to end, turn.

R3: Sl1p, purl to end, turn.

R4: Sl1k, knit to end, turn.

R5: Sl1p, purl to end, turn.

R6: Sl1k, knit to end, turn.

R7: Sl1p, purl to end, turn.

(Fig. 1)

Blue stitches representing picked-up stitches

Beg foot

R1: PM, this will become new beg of rnd. Knit across heel sts once more. Using new dpn, PU 5 sts from left side of heel flap, knit across half of held instep sts with same needle, knit across rest of held instep sts on third dpn, and PU 5 sts from right side of heel flap with same needle (fig. 2). (26 sts)

R2: Knit all sts.

R3: (K9, K2tog, K2tog) twice. (22 sts)

R4: Knit all sts.

R5: (K9, K2tog) twice. (20 sts)

R6–R19: Knit all sts.

R20: K2tog around. (10 sts)

Cut yarn and using tapestry needle, thread through rem sts to close foot.

Finishing

Are you ready to bring your monster to life? Turn to "General Monster Finishing Guidelines" on page 10 for detailed finishing directions.

Woohoo! A finished monster! It might be a good idea to get one of those cable-keeper things before you let Cecil loose in your house. However, from my personal experience it seems like they just prove to be a challenge for Cecil and he can still tangle the cords quite well. I just figure it's nice to have someone to blame for all the computer-cord knots and leave it at that.

Mouthy Monsters

Do you see how this Cecil's mouth line is a bit different than his brother's? This Cecil was so anxious to get a mouth he squirmed and squirmed while I was knitting to the point that I couldn't pick up stitches under both loops. I was forced to pick up stitches in the back loops only, which is why this Cecil has a more pronounced mouth. Sometimes you just have to let them do what they want to do!

(Fig. 2)

Picking up stitches on heel flap

Irving
the Icebox Monster

Irving is absolutely the life of the party. He's always smiling, laughing, and all around just being the most charming monster in the entire house. He currently lives in the icebox (as he calls it), or the refrigerator, so that he can snack on leftovers all day long. He's particularly fond of cheese trays and any wine coolers he can find, but he's not picky and will eat just about anything if he's hungry. Kat the kitchen monster (page 66) gets rather irritated with Irving since he tends to eat all of the components to her big gourmet meals. Maybe that's how Irving developed his charm skills—cooling down arguments with Kat!

Materials

It's easy to use any yarn-and-needle combination for this project. To find out more, see "What's the Deal with Gauge?" (page 5).

50–80 yards of yarn in main color (MC)
50–80 yards of yarn in contrasting color (CC)
1 set of double-pointed needles 2 or 3 sizes smaller than those recommended for yarn
Circular needle (36" or longer) in same size as dpns
Notions: tapestry needle, plastic safety eyes, white felt for teeth, fabric glue, stuffing, row counter (optional), stitch marker, straight pins (optional)

Samples

Purple-and-Green Irving

Finished size: 6" tall

MC 1 skein of Comfort from Berroco (50% super fine nylon, 50% super fine acrylic; 100 g/3.5 oz; 210 yds/193 m) in color 9728 [4]
CC 1 skein of Comfort from Berroco in color 9740
U.S. size 7 (4.5 mm) needles
12 mm black safety eyes

Green-and-Olive Irving

Finished size: 9" tall

MC 1 skein of Lana Grande from Cascade Yarns (100% Peruvian Highland wool; 100 g/3.5 oz; 87 yds) in color 6023 [6]
CC 1 skein of Lana Grande from Cascade Yarns in color 6041
U.S. size 13 (9 mm) needles
18 mm black safety eyes

Eye Patch

Using dpns, evenly CO 4 sts in CC and join, making sure not to twist sts. PM to indicate beg of rnd.

R1: K1f&b all sts. (8 sts)

R2: K1f&b all sts. (16 sts)

R3: Knit all sts.

R4: BO all sts pw

Body

Using Magic Loop method (page 6), evenly CO 45 sts in MC and join, making sure not to twist sts. PM to indicate beg of rnd.

R1–R26: Knit all sts.

R27: (K2tog, K3) around. (36 sts)

R28: Knit all sts.

R29: (K2tog, K2) around. (27 sts)

R30: Knit all sts.

R31: (K2tog, K1) around. (18 sts)

R32: Knit all sts.

R33: (K2tog) around. (9 sts)

Cut yarn and using tapestry needle, thread through rem sts to close head. Voila, monster beginnings! Go ahead and attach safety eyes now. Make sure to attach 1 eye *through* center of eye patch. With eye patch held down by eye, sew around it to attach it to face.

Base of Body

Work base in CC.

R1: Use dpns to PU 45 sts from CO edge of body (fig. 1). PM to indicate beg of rnd.

R2 and R3: Knit all sts.

R4: (K2tog, K3) around. (36 sts)

R5: (K2tog, K2) around. (27 sts)

R6: (K2tog, K1) around. (18 sts)

Stop and stuff Irving now.

R7: (K2tog) around. (9 sts)

Cut yarn and using tapestry needle, thread through rem sts to close base.

Ear (Make 2.)

Using dpns, evenly CO 8 sts in CC and join, making sure not to twist sts. PM to indicate beg of rnd.

R1: Knit all sts.

R2: (K1f&b, K3) twice. (10 sts)

R3: Knit all sts.

R4: (K4, K1f&b) twice. (12 sts)

R5: Knit all sts.

R6: (K1f&b, K5) twice. (14 sts)

R7: Knit all sts.

R8: (K6, K1f&b) twice. (16 sts)

R9–R12: Knit all sts.

Work 3-needle BO on all sts to close ear.

Foot (Make 2.)

Using dpns, evenly CO 12 sts in CC and join, making sure not to twist sts.

PM to indicate beg of rnd.

R1–R3: Knit all sts.

R4: (K1f&b, K5) twice. (14 sts)

R5: (K6, K1f&b) twice. (16 sts)

R6: (K1f&b, K7) twice. (18 sts)

R7: (K8, K1f&b) twice. (20 sts)

R8–R16: Knit all sts.

R17: (K2tog, K6, K2tog) twice. (16 sts)

R18: (K2tog, K4, K2tog) twice. (12 sts)

Turn foot inside out and work 3-needle BO on all sts. Turn foot RS out and start arms.

Arm (Make 2.)

Using dpns, evenly CO 10 sts in MC and join, making sure not to twist sts. PM to indicate beg of rnd.

R1–R15: Knit all sts.

Cut yarn and using tapestry needle, thread through rem sts to close hand.

Finishing

Are you ready to bring your monster to life? Turn to "General Monster Finishing Guidelines" on page 10 for detailed finishing directions.

Good job! You've completed not only a darling critter, but the most charming monster you'll ever meet. If you want to keep the peace in the kitchen, you could throw a party to celebrate Irving's completion, and serve all of Irving's favorite foods. Then Kat will have something to cook, and Irving will hopefully stop eating the components of her meals.

(Fig. 1)

Blue stitches representing picked-up stitches

Claude
the Closet Monster

Claude is the very typical monster that lives in a closet. Luckily Claude is absolutely the nicest monster around and if anyone is going to be living in your closet, Claude is the best guy to be in there. He's actually a huge chicken, which is why he tends to stay in the closet where it's dark and safe. Ironically enough, Claude is probably more afraid of kids than they are of the monster living in their closet!

Materials

It's easy to use any yarn-and-needle combination for this project.
To find out more, see "What's the Deal with Gauge?" (page 5).

120–175 yards of yarn

1 set of double-pointed needles 2 or 3 sizes smaller than those recommended for yarn

Circular needle (36" or longer) in same size as dpns

Notions: tapestry needle, plastic safety eyes, white felt for teeth, fabric glue, stuffing, row counter (optional), stitch marker, straight pins (optional)

Samples

Aqua Claude

Finished size: 12" tall

2 skeins of King George from Bristol Yarn Gallery (45% baby alpaca, 45% merino wool, 10% cashmere; 50 g; 105 yds) in color 1042 **(4)**

U.S. size 5 (3.75 mm) needles

9 mm black safety eyes

Green Claude

Finished size: 33" tall

2 skeins of Magnum from Cascade Yarns (100% Peruvian Highland wool; 250 g/8.82 oz; 123 yds) in color 9430 **(6)**

U.S. size 13 (9 mm) needles

12 mm black safety eyes

Body

Using circular needle, CO 20 sts. Do not join.

R1–R8: Beg with knit row, work back and forth in St st.

R9: Cont in St st and backward-loop CO 28 sts at end of row. Using Magic Loop method (page 6), join, making sure not to twist sts. PM to indicate beg of rnd.

R10–R30: Knit all sts.

R31: (K22, K2tog) twice. (46 sts)

R32: Knit all sts.

R33: (K2tog, K21) twice. (44 sts)

R34: Knit all sts.

R35: (K20, K2tog) twice. (42 sts)

R36: Knit all sts.

R37: (K2tog, K19) twice. (40 sts)

R38: Knit all sts.

R39: (K18, K2tog) twice. (38 sts)

R40: Knit all sts.

R41: (K2tog, K17) twice. (36 sts)

R42: Knit all sts.

R43: (K16, K2tog) twice. (34 sts)

R44: Knit all sts.

R45: (K2tog, K15) twice. (32 sts)

R46: Knit all sts.

R47: (K14, K2tog) twice. (30 sts)

R48: Knit all sts.

R49: (K2tog, K13) twice. (28 sts)

R50: Knit all sts.

R51: (K2tog, K10, K2tog) twice. (24 sts)

R52: Knit all sts.

R53: (K1f&b, K10, K1f&b) twice. (28 sts)

R54: Knit all sts.

R55: (K1f&b, K12, K1f&b) twice. (32 sts)

R56: Knit all sts.

R57: (K1f&b, K14, K1f&b) twice. (36 sts)

R58: Knit all sts.

R59: Knit the first 18 sts of the rnd, BO the last 18 sts.

R60: K18, PU 18 sts along the BO edge through both loops (fig. 1). The last 2 rnds create a line that will become Claude's mouth.

R61–R70: Knit all sts.

R71: (K2tog, K14, K2tog) twice. (32 sts)

R72: Knit all sts.

R73: (K2tog, K12, K2tog) twice. (28 sts)

R74: Knit all sts.

R75: (K2tog, K10, K2tog) twice. (24 sts)

R76: Knit all sts.

R77: (K2tog, K8, K2tog) twice. (20 sts)

R78: (K2tog, K6, K2tog) twice. (16 sts)

Turn Claude inside out and work 3-needle BO on all sts. Turn Claude RS out and keep knitting!

Arm (Make 2.)

Using dpns, evenly CO 6 sts and join, making sure not to twist sts. PM to indicate beg of rnd.

R1: K1f&b all sts. (12 sts)

R2: (K1, K1f&b) around. (18 sts)

R3–R6: Knit all sts.

R7: (K2tog, K7) twice. (16 sts)

R8: Knit all sts.

R9: (K6, K2tog) twice. (14 sts)

R10: Knit all sts.

R11: (K2tog, K5) twice. (12 sts)

R12: Knit all sts.

R13: (K4, K2tog) twice. (10 sts)

R14–R34: Knit all sts.

R35: BO all sts.

Leg (Make 2.)

Using dpns, evenly CO 12 sts and join, making sure not to twist sts. PM to indicate beg of rnd.

R1–R22: Knit all sts.

R23: K2tog, K2, K2tog, K6 to end. (10 sts)

R24: Knit all sts.

Place first 4 sts of rnd on 1 needle and next 6 sts on second needle.

Work heel with last 6 sts.

R1: Sl1p, purl to end, turn.

R2: Sl1k, knit to end, turn.

R3: Sl1p, purl to end, turn.

R4: Sl1k, knit to end, turn.

R5: Sl1p, purl to end, turn.

Beg foot

R1: PM, this will become new beg of rnd. Knit across heel sts once more. Using new dpn, PU 3 sts from left side of heel flap, knit across half of held instep sts with same needle, knit across rest of held instep sts on third dpn, and PU 3 sts from right side of heel flap with same needle (fig. 2). (16 sts)

R2: Knit all sts.

R3: (K6, K2tog) twice. (14 sts)

R4: Knit all sts.

R5: (K5, K2tog) twice. (12 sts)

R6–R15: Knit all sts.

R16: K2tog around. (6 sts)

(Fig. 1)

Blue stitches representing picked-up stitches

(Fig. 2)

Picking up stitches on heel flap

Cut yarn and using tapestry needle, thread through rem sts to close foot.

Finishing

Are you ready to bring your monster to life? Turn to "General Monster Finishing Guidelines" on page 10 for detailed finishing directions.

Sew up sides of base before attempting to attach legs so you know where center of base/body is going to be before you attach legs. Then, sew legs to flap edge to connect them and sew flap shut to finish up body. See fig. 2 on page 59.

You now have a completed closet monster! If you listen really hard you can hear me giving you a long-distance round of applause. You know, a closet monster might not be such a bad thing. You could encourage Claude to organize everything in there, and I don't think I'm the only one out there who is happy to have a monster guarding my shoes!

Resources

Contact the following yarn companies to find shops in your area that carry the yarns featured in this book.

Berroco
www.berroco.com
Comfort
Comfort Chunky
Pure Pima

Blue Sky Alpacas
http://blueskyalpacas.com
Dyed Cotton

Bristol Yarn Gallery
www.plymouthyarn.com
King George

Cascade Yarn
www.cascadeyarns.com
220 Wool
220 Superwash
Cash Vero
Lana Grande
Magnum
220 Heathers
Pastaza

Classic Elite Yarns
www.classiceliteyarns.com
Classic Elite: Ariosa
Classic Elite: Montera
Verde Collection: Sprout

Lorna's Laces
www.lornaslaces.net
Fisherman
Shepherd Bulky
Shepherd Worsted

Plymouth Yarn Company Inc.
www.plymouthyarn.com
Baby Alpaca Grande
Mulberry Merino

Spud and Chloë
www.spudandchloe.com
Outer
Sweater

Safety Eyes
Safety eyes can be found in most major craft stores or many places online; my favorite place is www.6060.etsy.com.

Abbreviations and Glossary

( ) Work instructions within parentheses as many times as directed

beg begin(ning)

BO bind off

CC contrasting color

CO cast on

cont continue(ing)

dpn(s) double-pointed needle(s)

inc increase(s)

join begin to knit in the round

K knit

K2tog knit 2 stitches together—1 stitch decreased

K1f&b knit into front and back of same stitch—1 stitch increased

MC main color

P purl

PM place marker

PU pick up and knit

pw purlwise

R round

rem remain(ing)

rnd(s) round(s)

RS right side

sl1k slip 1 stitch knitwise

sl1p slip 1 stitch purlwise

st(s) stitch(es)

St st stockinette stitch

tog together

You might also enjoy these other fine titles from

Martingale & Company

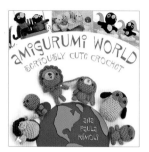

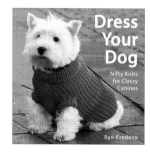

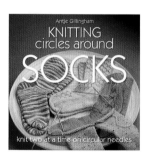

Our books are available at bookstores and your favorite craft, fabric, and yarn retailers. Visit us at www.martingale-pub.com or contact us at:

1-800-426-3126

International: 1-425-483-3313
Fax: 1-425-486-7596
Email: info@martingale-pub.com